Countertraditions in the Bible

Countertraditions in the Bible

A Feminist Approach

Ilana Pardes

Harvard University Press
Cambridge, Massachusetts
London, England

Copyright © 1992 by the President and Fellows of Harvard College
All rights reserved
Printed in the United States of America
10 9 8 7 6 5 4 3 2

First Harvard University Press paperback edition, 1993

Library of Congress Cataloging-in-Publication Data
Pardes, Ilana.
Countertraditions in the Bible : a feminist approach
/ Ilana Pardes.
p.   cm.
Includes bibliographical references and index.
ISBN 0-674-17542-5 (alk. paper) (cloth)
ISBN 0-674-17545-X (pbk.)
1. Women in the Bible.   2. Bible.   O.T.—Criticism,
interpretation, etc.   I. Title.
BS575.P27   1992
220.9′2—dc20   91-40975
[B]   CIP

For Itamar and for Keren

Acknowledgments

This book is in a sense a dialogue between Berkeley and Jerusalem. It had its beginnings as a doctoral dissertation at the University of California, Berkeley. I am most grateful to Robert Alter for his insightful criticisms, admirable openness, ongoing support, and for introducing me to biblical literature through his inspiring courses and books. I have an equal debt to Chana Kronfeld, who has always been my role model for what a teacher and a scholar should be. Her friendship and extraordinary help have been invaluable. My thanks also go to Elizabeth Abel, who lured me into the world of feminist theory and helped in shaping my own approach to it.

Later, at the Hebrew University of Jerusalem, I found more help and support than I ever hoped for. By far my greatest debt is to Ruth Nevo, who gave so generously of her time and encouraged me to dare tackle some of the most obscure passages in the Bible. Her brilliant comments have been a continual source of inspiration. I have a special intellectual and personal indebtedness to Gidi Nevo, whose remarkable aesthetic sensitivity and keen criticisms enabled me to expand on points about which I was sure I had said all that I possibly could. I am very much indebted to Moshe Greenberg for making me realize that biblical scholarship had much to offer my research. I also wish to thank Shalom Paul for guiding my reading in the field of biblical studies.

I made final touches on the book at Princeton, where I have benefited greatly from the instructive comments and warm support of my friends and colleagues. I am particularly grateful to Mark Cohen, Maria DiBattista, John Gager, Robert Gibbs, Robert Fagles, Martha Himmelfarb, Alicia Ostriker, Avrom Udovitch, and Froma Zeitlin.

It is a distinct pleasure to express my deep gratitude to my students at Berkeley, Jerusalem, and Princeton. Stimulating contact with them has been an important source of criticisms and suggestions.

Many other people helped me tremendously somewhere along the road: Michal Aviad, Mieke Bal, Daniel Boyarin, David Damrosch, Ruth Ginsburg, Bluma Goldstein, Zali Gurevich, Raaya Kalinholf, Tsipora Peskin, Naomi Seidman, Meir Wigoder, Shimshon Wigoder, and my parents. Many thanks to Ann Louise McLaughlin at Harvard University Press for her sensitive and meticulous editing and to Nita Schechet, Judy Levi, and Amy Pierce for their help in proofreading. For financial assistance, I am indebted to the Memorial Foundation for Jewish Culture, the Herczeg Scholarship, and the Lady Davis Fellowship.

My book is dedicated to Itamar Lurie whom I met, of all places, at the foothills of Mount Sinai. I cannot imagine what it would have been like to write this work without his love and encouragement. It is also dedicated to Keren, whose birth has added so much light to our life.

I.P.

Contents

Countertraditions in the Bible

❦ 1 ❧

Preliminary Excavations

Very deep is the well of the past. Should we not call it bottomless? Bottomless indeed, if—and perhaps only if—the past we mean is the past merely of the life of mankind, that riddling essence of which our own normally unsatisfied and quite abnormally wretched existences form a part; whose mystery, of course, includes our own and is the alpha and omega of all our questions, lending burning immediacy to all we say, and significance to all our striving. For the deeper we sound, the further down into the lower world of the past we probe and press, the more do we find that the earliest foundations of humanity, its history and culture, reveal themselves unfathomable. No matter to what hazardous lengths we let out our line they still withdraw again, and further, into the depths. Again and further are the right words, for the unresearchable plays a kind of mocking game with our researching ardours; it offers apparent holds and goals, behind which, when we have gained them, new reaches of the past still open out.

—Thomas Mann, *Joseph and His Brothers*

The well of the past, as Thomas Mann beautifully puts it, lures us to probe and explore its depths, promising "significance to all our striving," a beginning and an end to all our questions. And yet the further we go back in time, the more we realize that the past is a "bottomless" well, which can only frustrate our desire to retrieve lost depths. This quest turns out to be all the more frustrating when the voices we wish to draw up from the past are voices of women whose words were only rarely recorded. The expedition then becomes, I would suggest, far more archaeological in character; it involves a search for mutilated ruins and relics scattered about. It requires, much like the psychoanalytic reconstruction of the past, a hermeneutics which cautiously follows the traces of repression in an attempt to uncover buried scenes.[1]

In my effort to retrieve the biblical past, I oscillate between a disturbing suspicion that this well is quite empty insofar as female sources are concerned and a fascination with the unexpected ways in which antipatriarchal perspectives have been partially preserved, against all odds, in the canon. Accordingly, my analyses entail both an examination of the marks of patriarchal modes of censorship and an attempt to reconstruct, in light of the surviving remains, antithetical undercurrents which call into question the monotheistic repression of femininity. I try, in other words, to avoid an all too common tendency of feminist critics to turn the remote past into the fulfillment of current dreams. This does not mean that the present has no bearing on my endeavors. Quite the contrary. Like any hermeneutic pursuit, my own pursuit entails an attempt to make sense of the present in light of the past, to explore a distant mystery which includes our own. I try, however, to engage in a dialogue with the past without idealizing it. I strive to listen to the otherness of past voices, though I realize, with Stephen Greenblatt (1988:1), that in our most intense moments of straining to listen to the dead, it is often our own voices that we hear.

Two major trends of feminist biblical criticism are challenged in my book. The one trend, whose prominent representative is Phyllis Trible, seeks to "depatriarchalize" biblical texts. In her seminal work, *God and the Rhetoric of Sexuality* (1978), Trible sets the ground for an alternative feminist hermeneutics of Scripture, but her readings of the Bible turn out to be most problematic insofar as they efface its patriarchal stamp and endorse an idyllic reconciliation between "Biblical faith and women's liberation" (1976:218). I equally criticize the opposite trend, the approach of feminist critics such as Esther Fuchs who focus solely on the patriarchal presuppositions of biblical representations of female characters. Both approaches have similar drawbacks: their ahistorical examination of the Bible, and their homogenization of its striking diversity.

My readings call for a consideration of the heterogeneity of the Hebrew canon, for an appreciation of the variety of socio-ideological horizons evident in this composite text. The contribution of nineteenth-century German biblical scholarship, that is, of Higher Criticism, in exposing this heterogeneity cannot be overestimated.[2] In an impressive demystification of the origin of Scriptures, Higher Criticism shattered the traditional notion of the Bible as the Word of God, treating it as a composite work whose history may be examined like any other ancient text. Through an analysis of stylistic features, narrative consistency, and theological approach, "higher critics" identified four principal strata in the Pentateuch: the Yahwistic Document (J), presumably the earliest source, dating back to the tenth century B.C.E.; the Elohistic Document (E), from approximately the ninth century B.C.E.; the Deuteronomistic Document (D), which might date back to the seventh century B.C.E.; and the Priestly Document (P), the latest source, considered to be representative of priestly traditions from the sixth and fifth centuries B.C.E.

The "documentary hypothesis," once taken to be a historical truth, has been criticized in the past few decades from various directions. First, the speculative character of Higher Criticism's findings (and datings in particular) has been laid bare. Second, it has been challenged from a literary perspective. Thus, Robert Alter, in his groundbreaking *The Art of Biblical Narrative* (1981), aptly criticizes biblical scholarship for its "atomism," for its lack of attention to the intricate interrelations between biblical strands, its failure to take into account biblical poetics.

I would like to add yet another critique by using Bakhtin's observations concerning heterogeneity. In his challenge to traditional notions of unity, Bakhtin is, in a sense, a follower of Higher Criticism (see Hartman 1986:13). Yet unlike his precursors, he does not set limits to textual diversity. Language, for Bakhtin, "at any given moment of its historical existence . . . is heteroglot from top to bottom: it represents the co-existence of socio-ideological contradictions between the present and the past, between differing epochs of the past, between different socio-ideological groups in the present, between tendencies, schools, circles and so forth, all given a bodily form. These 'languages' of heteroglossia intersect each other in a variety of ways, forming new socially typifying 'languages'" (1981:291).

The Bible is far more of a heteroglot text than Higher Criticism would have it. The stratification which biblical scholars have offered is a good point of departure, but it does not suffice. What Higher Criticism didn't dream of dealing with (nor did Bakhtin for that matter) is the gender code, or rather the possibility of friction between heterogeneous perceptions of femininity. My goal is to explore the tense dialogue between the dominant patriarchal discourses of the Bible and counter female voices which attempt to put forth other truths. In some cases I trace these antithetical voices in texts such as "The Bridegroom of Blood" (Exod. 4) or the Song of Songs, which often have been defined as deviant but rarely from a feminist perspective. In other cases I try to tease out the antithetical character of stories or subplots whose otherness has been overlooked by biblical exegetes. In most chapters I sharpen the antithetical features of these exceptional texts through an intertextual analysis. Thus I consider the Priestly story of creation as a reinterpretation of the Yahwistic one, the Book of Ruth as an antithetical completion of Genesis, and the Song of Songs as a critique of the prophetic representations of the amorous bond between God and the nation.

Needless to say, my own study is only a partial account of biblical heteroglossia; it is an attempt to present a heterogeneity that hitherto has been mostly overlooked. I should add, however, that although I focus on biblical representations of femininity, I attempt to sketch the ways in which antithetical female voices intermingle with other repressed elements in the Bible, primarily polytheistic elements, but also skeptical voices, anticovenantal currents, and erotic longings.

I examine these dialogues by means of an interdisciplinary approach, relying on feminist theory, literary criticism, biblical scholarship, and psychoanalysis, setting these disciplines at times against each other in order to expose inevitable points of tension. This theoretical heterogeneity, I think, contributes to the understanding of the character and function of the countertraditions I wish to explore.

My work owes much to Mieke Bal's brilliant trilogy: *Lethal Love* (1987), *Murder and Difference* (1988a), and *Death and Dissymmetry* (1988b). Bal brought to biblical feminist criticism a refreshing interdisciplinary approach, whose intricacies I discuss in detail in the following chapter. It will suffice to say in the meantime, by way of introduction, that I find her narratological method of opening the text to other "subject positions" as well as her semiotic critique of the monolithically misogynist view of biblical interpretations most intriguing and powerful. I also agree with her claim that a historical consideration of biblical texts can only invigorate the critical gesture of feminist readings of the Bible.

I have, however, two reservations. First, Bal's insightful readings of biblical narrative occasionally turn out to be anachronistic. This is particularly evident at points where Bal uncritically uses Christian concepts in her analyses. The

Original Fall, like the association of sin and sexuality—two notions which Bal relies on in her reading of Genesis 2–3—are foreign to the Hebrew Bible. Her anachronism is also apparent in a lack of attention to the influence of polytheistic texts—Mesopotamian and Egyptian mythologies in particular—on biblical figurations of femininity.

Second, I find Bal's association of reading strategies with given ideologies problematic. I do not mean to suggest that interpretive methods are innocent of an ideological base, but rather that the interrelations between the two are far more complex than Bal would have it. This tendency becomes jarring when Bal defines Trible's work as sexist ("despite its feminist intentions"), while valorizing Lacan's brief analysis of Hugo's interpretation of the Book of Ruth. Although Lacan's reading of the Book of Ruth undermines the antithetical representation of female heroism in this text by foregrounding Boaz's needs, it is curiously presented in *Lethal Love* as a nonsexist interpretation. It is in fact the only reading Bal does not criticize in her keen analysis of modern reception of biblical texts.

Miriam and Her Brothers

As a preliminary presentation of my excavative mode of analysis, I will examine the history of Miriam the prophetess, Moses' sister. Unlike the story of "Shakespeare's sister," Virginia Woolf's brilliant creation, the fate of Moses' sister does not have to be invented.[3] Her deeds are recorded in the history of the house of Israel.

Miriam's story, however, is very brief, fragmentary, and scattered.[4] She first appears in Exodus 2:4. Her name is not mentioned. Defined as Moses' sister, she stands at a distance, watching over the ark of her baby brother as it lies afloat on the Nile, hidden among the reeds. She reappears in Exodus 2:7–8, where she cunningly talks Pharaoh's daughter into employing a Hebrew woman as Moses' nurse. While Moses grows up at Pharaoh's palace and exerts his burgeoning powers, first in slaying an Egyptian and later in bargaining with Pharaoh, we hear nothing of Miriam. Nor is she mentioned in the detailed descriptions of the various preparations for the exodus. Upon the crossing of the Red Sea, she bursts out with a name and a title, leading the women in song and dance: "And Miriam the prophetess, the sister of Aaron, took a timbrel in her hand; and all the women went out after her with timbrels and with dances. And Miriam answered them, Sing ye to the Lord" (Exod. 15:20–21).[5] But her career as a leading poet is curtailed. She disappears from the picture for the rest of Exodus and is never mentioned in Leviticus.

In the midst of the wanderings in the wilderness, in Numbers 12, Miriam turns up again in a story which does not have a prominent status in the collective memory. It is not recounted in children's Bibles, nor has it been a topic for literary or artistic interpretations.[6] Why do readers rarely remember this episode? I will attempt to tackle this question later on. Let us first recollect this piece.

And Miriam and Aaron spake against Moses because of the Ethiopian woman whom he had married: for he had married an Ethiopian woman. And they said, Hath the Lord indeed spoken only by Moses? hath he not spoken also by us? And the Lord heard it. (Now the man Moses was very meek, above all the men which were upon the face of the earth.) And the Lord spake suddenly unto Moses, and unto Aaron, and unto Miriam, Come out ye three unto the tabernacle of the congregation. And they three came out. And the Lord came down in the pillar of the cloud, and stood in the door of the tabernacle, and called Aaron and Miriam: and they both came forth. And He said, Hear now my words: If there be a prophet among you, I the Lord will make myself known unto him in a vision, and will speak unto him in a dream. My servant Moses is not so, who is faithful in all mine house. With him will I speak

mouth to mouth, even apparently, and not in dark speeches;
and the similitude of the Lord shall he behold: wherefore then
were ye not afraid to speak against my servant Moses? And the
anger of the Lord was kindled against them; and he departed.
And the cloud departed from off the tabernacle; and, behold,
Miriam became leprous, white as snow: And Aaron looked
upon Miriam, and, behold, she was leprous. And Aaron said
unto Moses, Alas, my lord, I beseech thee, lay not the sin upon
us, wherein we have done foolishly, and wherein we have
sinned. Let her not be as one dead, of whom the flesh is half
consumed when he cometh out of his mother's womb. And
Moses cried unto the Lord, saying, Heal her now, O God, I
beseech thee. And the Lord said unto Moses, If her father had
but spit in her face, should she not be ashamed seven days? let
her be shut out from the camp seven days, and after that let
her be received in again. And Miriam was shut out from the
camp seven days: and the people journeyed not till Miriam was
brought in again. And afterward the people removed from
Hazeroth, and pitched in the wilderness of Paran.   (Num. 12)

This chapter poses reading difficulties which are not
uncommon in biblical texts. The first verse, dealing with the
reservations of Miriam and Aaron with respect to Moses'
Cushite wife, is most obscure. We do not know whether or
not this Cushite wife was Zipporah, nor do we know why
Miriam and Aaron were critical of the marriage. The following verse sheds no light on these matters for it raises an
entirely different issue: the respective status of the siblings
vis-à-vis God. Biblical scholarship has suggested that
Numbers 12 consists of two different Yahwistic traditions
(see Noth 1968:92–97) which have been combined, because
both deal with complaints on the part of Miriam and Aaron
against Moses' conduct.

Perhaps the first strand is meant to present yet another
story of female rivalry, cognate with the stories of Sarah and
Hagar, or Rachel and Leah. But Aaron's participation in this

scene (even if he is not the principal instigator, as seems indicated by the order in which the siblings are presented in 12:1
and the fact that the verb "spake against" appears in the feminine singular form) and particularly the foreign origin of the
Cushite wife point to other possible plots. All in all, this verse
is far too nebulous and fragmentary to lend itself to a plausible interpretation.

Luckily the second strand offers a more substantial
drama, the kind Gerald Bruns (1984) would call a "canonization story." "Hath the Lord indeed spoken only by Moses?"
Miriam and Aaron ask, protesting against the privileged status of Moses' discourse. Their discourses too, they seem to
claim, should be considered as authoritative and binding.
They too, not unlike Moses, have been speaking under divine
inspiration. Moses does not reply. Instead, God intervenes in
this drama of sibling rivalry, reaffirms His favoritism, chastises the two rebels, and ends up striking Miriam with leprosy
for seeking an equal footing with Moses. Exclusion from the
canon is not necessarily a female issue, and yet the fact that
Miriam is punished while Aaron is spared suggests that the
Law has even less sympathy for oppositional female voices.

God's punishment of Miriam is strikingly harsh, so
much so that Aaron pleads on her behalf. Having learned a
lesson about canonical hierarchies, however, he addresses
Moses instead of God: "Let her not be as one dead, of whom
the flesh is half consumed when he cometh out of his mother's womb" (12:12). If Miriam plays a maternal role both in
watching over Moses in Exodus 2 and later, on a national
level, in her leading of the women in Exodus 15, the leprosy,
as Aaron's simile makes clear, reverses her position. The
mother figure of the nation becomes as a child, even a dead
child, or aborted fetus, whose flesh is eaten away.

In response to Moses' intercession, God justifies His
punishment, reiterating the belittling of Miriam, for she is
now compared to a shameful daughter. "And the Lord said

unto Moses, If her father had but spit in her face, should she
not be ashamed seven days? let her be shut out from the camp
seven days" (12:14). The analogy God draws is quite
astounding. Miriam's demand for greater expression seems to
be synonymous with lewdness, and leprosy turns out to be
the punitive spitting of the Father.

    Although Miriam is brought back to the camp after
being "shut out" for seven days, she dies shortly after this
harsh incident without uttering an additional word. "Then
came the children of Israel, even the whole congregation, into
the desert of Zin . . . and Miriam died there, and was buried
there" (Num. 20:1). For in Moses' day a woman with the gift
of prophecy would have had to be silenced and then buried
in the wilderness for daring to demand a central cultural
position.

    Numbers 12 clearly reaffirms the patriarchal presuppo-
sitions of the canon, and yet it offers an account of an antithetical approach to cultural dynamics, to the hegemonic
character of Moses' discourse. Let me suggest that if this passage about Miriam's pursuit of canonical power hasn't
enjoyed a privileged status in the collective memory—in clear
contradistinction to the scenes by the Nile and at the Red
Sea—it is precisely because female protest, even when it is
put down, is far from palatable. Or perhaps we witness here
a common inclination in biblical reception to simplify the
brief histories of female characters, to attribute to them either
a positive role or a "negative" one. Most biblical exegetes
have emphasized Miriam's contribution to national liberation, which is probably why her rebellious move in Numbers
12 has been overlooked.

    The heterogeneity that marks Miriam's characterization
is, however, manifested in the striking differences between
the *biblical* commemorations of Miriam. She is presented in
the Deuteronomistic law on lepers as an exemplary outcast.
"Take heed in the plague of leprosy, that thou observe dili-

gently, and do according to all that the priests the Levites shall teach you: as I commanded them, so ye shall observe to do. Remember what the Lord thy God did unto Miriam by the way, after that ye were come forth out of Egypt" (24:8–9). Conversely, in Micah 6:4 she is mentioned (after Moses and Aaron) as a national liberator: "For I brought thee up out of the Land of Egypt, and redeemed thee out of the house of servants; and I sent before thee Moses, Aaron, and Miriam."

What then do these scattered pieces of Miriam's story add up to? No whole, to be sure. Miriam's title of prophetess, the audacity with which she demands to be heard, the severity of her punishment, and her appearance on Micah's list of national deliverers (despite the order of presentation) all create an impression that her role was far greater than recorded, that there must have been other traditions which were not included in the canon.[7] One should bear in mind that noncanonical texts such as the Book of the Yashar, the Book of the Battles of Yahweh, and the Chronicles of the Kings of Judea are in fact mentioned in the Bible.[8] These titles may not sound too promising as far as women's histories are concerned, but they serve as evidence of the corpus of ancient Hebrew literature which has been lost.

Lacking the acumen and courage of Indiana Jones, one cannot hope to unearth lost noncanonical texts. But much can be done merely by probing within the canon itself. I have tried to illustrate how one can find antithetical female voices by paying attention to underexamined fragments on the margins of biblical historiography. My reading thus entails a reversal of canonical hierarchies, for I have foregrounded Miriam's pursuit and marginalized Moses' discourse. It is, however, no more biased than interpretations which adhere to the canonical order and overlook the traces of repressed voices in the Bible. Psychoanalysis has taught us that the impact of the repressed on our past as well as on our present need not be undermined. However tentative such hermeneutic adventures may be, they can, I think, shed light both on the beginnings of Western cultural institutions and on the mutilated, though priceless, remnants of past voices which have paved the way for current feminist critiques of cultural dynamics.

★ ❧2❧

Creation according to Eve

Before embarking on other hermeneutic expeditions within the biblical text, I would like to provide a more extensive survey of the various feminist approaches to the Bible. I have chosen to introduce these approaches through a contrastive analysis of six feminist readings of the story (or stories) of the creation of woman in Genesis. No feminist critic dealing with the Bible has resisted the temptation to discuss the opening chapters of Genesis, the very base of Western perception of femininity, which is why I use this text as a point of comparison. My analysis, by no means exhaustive, is meant primarily to present the different questions feminist biblical criticism has raised from its beginnings in the nineteenth century until today, to show from the outset that there is no single monolithic feminist approach to Scripture.

Elizabeth Cady Stanton

Elizabeth Cady Stanton was the editor of *The Woman's Bible,* a book commonly regarded as the forerunner of feminist biblical criticism. In the late 1880s Stanton, the organizer of the first women's rights convention, held at Seneca Falls in 1848, and the author of the demand for women's suffrage, set out to compile a series of critical commentaries on biblical passages which mentioned or affected women.[1] For her, this was an indispensable political act against an "enemy," which until then suffragists had failed to confront: organized religion. Few women scholars were willing to participate in this audacious anticlerical project, and, although Stanton eventually managed to recruit five contributors, most of the commentaries were her own. *The Woman's Bible* was finally published in 1895 and 1898, creating an uproar. It was condemned both by clergymen who regarded the book as "the work of women and the devil" (Stanton, 1985:II,7) and by the members of the National American Woman Suffrage Association, which by then was unwilling to risk antagonism and hurt the campaign for suffrage.[2]

In the face of such criticism, Stanton wittily argues that "His Satanic Majesty . . . has been so busy of late years attending Synods, General Assemblies and Conferences, to prevent the recognition of women delegates" (ibid.) that he has had no time to participate in the project. Insisting on the great value of *The Woman's Bible,* she explains in a letter to *The Critic* that the book

> comes to the ordinary reader like a real benediction. It tells her that the good Lord did not write the Book; that the garden scene is a fable: that she is in no way responsible for the laws of the universe. The Christian scholars and scientists will not tell her this, for they see she is the key to the situation. Take the snake, the fruit tree and the woman from the tableau, and we have no fall, no frowning Judge, no Inferno, no everlasting punishment—hence no need of a Savior. Thus the bottom falls out of the whole Christian theology. Here is the reason why in all the Biblical researches and higher criticisms, the scholars never touch the position of woman.[3]

Although Stanton rails against Higher Criticism for neglecting to deal with the position of women, it is precisely this new historical approach to the Bible—which became influential in the American academy by the 1880s—that made her attack on the "bottom" of theology possible, for once the belief in the divine origin of the Bible was shattered and Holy Writ was treated like any other ancient text, its authority in the matter of woman's nature and sphere could be called into question (see Gifford 1985:22). The iconoclastic "benediction" Stanton thus offers the readers of *The Woman's Bible* is a feminist adaptation of Higher Criticism. "We have made a fetich of the Bible long enough" (1985:II,8), she argues, calling for a critical examination of the Bible's role in the degradation of women in Western culture.

Despite the pronounced irreverance of the *The Woman's Bible,* Stanton is interested not only in challenging biblical tenets; she also attempts to highlight those biblical elements which teach "love, charity, liberty, justice and equality for all the human family" (1985:I,12). Hence, she accepts passages upon which a "rational religion" (DuBois 1981:228–229), compatible with Enlightenment liberalism, could be developed. In a frequently quoted passage Stanton concludes: "The Bible cannot be accepted or rejected as a whole, its teachings are varied and its lessons differ widely from each other. In criticising the peccadilloes of Sarah, Rebecca and Rachel, we would not shadow the virtues of Deborah, Huldah and Vashti" (I,13).

Stanton's commentary on the opening chapters of Genesis is a fine example of her approach. Relying on the findings of Higher Criticism, she points out that there are two contradictory stories of creation: the Priestly tradition (Gen. 1–2:3), where the creation of man and woman is depicted as simultaneous and egalitarian ("So God created man in his image . . . male and female created He them" [1:27]), and the Yahwistic tradition (Gen. 2:4–3), where woman is presented as "a mere afterthought . . . The only reason for her advent being the solitude of man" (I,20). For Stanton, the Priestly version is the only acceptable one: "The

equal position declared in the first account must prove more
satisfactory to both sexes; created alike in the image of God—
the Heavenly Mother and Father" (I,21). Accordingly, she
calls on her readers to reject the second account, which she
defines as the work of some "wily writer" who, "seeing the
perfect equality of man and woman in the first chapter, felt it
important for the dignity and dominion of man to effect
woman's subordination in some way" (ibid.).

To reinforce her argument, Stanton compares the respective modes of representation in Genesis 1 and 2. She regards
the Priestly account as a refined realist representation—"in
harmony with science, common sense, and the experience of
mankind in natural laws"—and the story of the Garden of
Eden as a "mere allegory," a text devoid of truth (snakes
obviously cannot speak, Darwin's theory of evolution is far
more convincing than the Yahwistic depiction of the development of the first pair, and so on). There is, in other words,
a clear correlation between ideology and aesthetics: the
enlightened account embraces realism, while the sexist
account is a reactionary allegory of no social or literary value.
In Stanton's words, "There is something sublime in bringing
order out of chaos; light out of darkness; giving each planet
its place in the solar system; oceans and lands their limits;
wholly inconsistent with a petty surgical operation, to find
material for the mother of the race. It is on this allegory that
all the enemies of women rest their battering rams, to prove
her inferiority" (I,20).

Her valorization of the first account of the creation of
woman needs to be seen against the background of the con-
sistent favoring of the Yahwistic account in Western culture.
What Stanton makes clear is that Genesis 2 has been favored
primarily because of its compatibility with patriarchal values.[4] Her feminist hermeneutics thus reverses the relation of
margins and center. In *The Woman's Bible* the rather unknown

account of the creation of woman becomes the authoritative one.

In her attack on the misogynist passages in the Bible, in her ridiculing of traditional biblical interpretations, and in her attempts to account for the heterogeneous representations of women in the Bible, Stanton's work prefigures the sundry readings of the Bible by twentieth-century feminist critics. But one should bear in mind the project's weaknesses. First, Stanton's limited familiarity with Higher Criticism leads her at times to draw mistaken conclusions. Thus her suggestion that the "wily writer" of Genesis 2 attempted to undermine the egalitarian approach offered in Genesis 1 is incompatible with the findings of Higher Criticism. That is, the Yahwistic Document predates the Priestly account, even though the latter appears first in the text. Second, her assumptions concerning the interrelations of ideology and aesthetics tend to be naive and simplistic.

Simone de Beauvoir and Kate Millett

With the reemergence of the women's movement in the last third of the twentieth century, the question of the Bible's role in the degradation of women was raised once again. In the first major works of feminist criticism—Simone de Beauvoir's *The Second Sex* (1949) and Kate Millett's *Sexual Politics* (1969)—the Bible is condemned as one of the founding texts of patriarchy. Insofar as de Beauvoir and Millett expose and criticize the patriarchal presuppositions of the Bible, they follow in Stanton's footsteps, endowing their precursor's insights with a more solid theoretical base. And yet, unlike Stanton, they clearly have no interest in forming a "rational religion" or highlighting progressive biblical passages. Their focus on the patriarchal facets of the Bible, however, need not be attributed solely to their secular bent, for

the primary objective of what is known today as the first
wave of feminist criticism is to lay bare the misogyny of male
traditions. It is only in the third wave of feminist criticism
that the heterogeneity of male writings becomes a legitimate
research topic.[5]

Let me stress that neither de Beauvoir nor Millett set out
to provide an extensive critique of biblical texts. The only
text both choose to discuss (briefly) is the Yahwistic one.
Their choice is not accidental. Genesis 1 does not lend itself
as easily to an examination of stereotypical images of women.

De Beauvoir uses the story of the creation of woman
from Adam's rib to corroborate her thesis concerning woman's status as Other.

> Eve was not fashioned at the same time as the man; she was
> not fabricated from a different substance, nor of the same clay
> as was used to model Adam: she was taken from the flank of
> the first male. Not even her birth was independent; God did
> not spontaneously choose to create her as an end in herself and
> in order to be worshipped directly by her in return for it. She
> was destined by Him for man; it was to rescue Adam from
> loneliness that He gave her to him, in her mate was her origin
> and her purpose; she was his complement on the order of the
> inessential. Thus she appeared in the guise of privileged prey.
> She was nature elevated to transparency of consciousness; she
> was a conscious being, but naturally submissive. And therein
> lies the wondrous hope that man has often put in woman: he
> hopes to fulfill himself as a being by carnally possessing a
> being, but at the same time confirming his sense of freedom
> through the docility of a free person.   (1952:159–160)

Woman is thus the "dream incarnated," the perfect Other
who serves as an intermediary between man and nature,
enabling Adam to define himself as Subject. Conveniently,
woman's subjecthood is never at stake; she remains the "ines-
sential who never goes back to being the essential." In de

Beauvoir's analysis of Genesis 2, details such as the order of creation, the material from which Eve was made, and Adam's preference for a woman over animals are thus convincingly set within an existential-feminist framework.

Kate Millett focuses on the implied association of woman, sex, and guilt in this text, or the traditional Christian perception of the Fall.

> Patriarchy has God on its side. One of its most effective agents of control is the powerfully expeditious character of its doctrines as to the nature and origin of the female and the attribution to her alone of the dangers and evils it imputes to sexuality . . . Patriarchal religion and ethics tend to lump the female and sex together as if the whole burden of the onus and stigma it attaches to sex were the fault of the female alone . . . To blame the evils and sorrows of life—loss of Eden and the rest—on sexuality, would all too logically implicate the male, and such implication is hardly the purpose of the story, designed as it is expressly in order to blame all this world's discomfort on the female. (1969:72–75)

Millett goes on to suggest that in this account of "how humanity invented sexual intercourse" (p. 74), Adam is exempted from sexual guilt, for the serpent represents the phallus in the initial sexual move. In other words, the sexual drive of man is displaced (or transferred to the serpent) in a way which makes Eve the culpable seductress. What Millett criticizes harshly is the Bible's negative attitude toward woman, which is inseparable from its condemnation of sexuality.

The work of de Beauvoir and Millett is representative of the limited interest feminist critics outside the domain of religious studies have had in the Bible up until the mid-1980s. Although the examination of the patriarchal base of Greek mythology has been a principal endeavor of feminist criticism all along, the Bible—except for the story of Eve—has remained mostly untouchable because of its status as a "religious text." Dealing with biblical texts extensively was in a sense perceived as an affirmation of the Bible's authority. The rise of the second wave of feminist criticism in the late 1970s, with its focus on female texts, did not bring about much change in this respect.

Phyllis Trible

Within the domain of religous studies feminist discussions of religion have flourished from the seventies on. Most of the important books pertaining to this trend, such as Mary Daly's *Beyond God the Father* (1973) and Rosemary Radford Ruether's *Sexism and God-Talk* (1983), deal primarily with theological issues rather than with textual analysis; as such they remain outside the scope of my discussion. Phyllis Trible, whose work I will discuss at length, is one of the few feminist biblical scholars who has applied literary theory (New Criticism in particular) to the Hebrew Bible.[6] Her scholarly and comprehensive study of biblical texts is an important landmark, although it lacks what Mieke Bal defines as "contemporary theoretical reflection" (1986:73).

In "Depatriarchalizing in Biblical Interpretation," her most influential article, Trible challenges the assumptions of the first wave of feminist criticism, refuting Kate Millett's claim that "Patriarchy has God on its side."

> The women's movement errs when it dismisses the Bible as inconsequential or condemns it as enslaving. In rejecting Scripture women ironically accept male chauvinistic interpretations and thereby capitulate to the very view they are protesting. But there is another way: to reread (not rewrite) the Bible without the blinders of Israelite men or of Paul, Barth, Bonhoeffer, and a host of others. The hermeneutical challenge is to translate Biblical faith without sexism.   (1976:218)

Trible's depatriarchalization of biblical criticism has been her most significant contribution to feminist criticism of the Bible. She has outlined a way of undoing misogynist readings of the Bible which is far more refined than Stanton's brief commentaries. And yet the fact that Trible remains on God's side—exempting Yahweh from critique—makes her approach problematic. Elisabeth Schüssler Fiorenza criticizes Trible for her neo-orthodox theology, claiming that "a biblical theology that does not seriously confront 'the patriarchal stamp' of the Bible and its religious-political legitimization of the patriarchal oppression of women is in danger of using a feminist perspective to rehabilitate the authority of the Bible, rather than to rehabilitate women's biblical history and theological heritage" (1983:21).

It comes as no surprise that the first account of creation is of great importance in Trible's work. In "Clues in the Text," her theoretical introductory chapter to *God and the Rhetoric of Sexuality,* she regards Genesis 1:27 as the primary scriptural clue for the subject of God and the rhetoric of sexuality. Trible suggests that "the formal parallelism between the phrases 'in the image of God' and 'male and female' indicates a semantic correspondence between a lesser known element and a better known element" (1978:17). Implicitly, then, metaphor becomes the chosen trope, with the image of God as the tenor and human sexuality as vehicle. By turning this parallelism into a guiding metaphor, Trible highlights the pluralism and equality that God's image suggests, refuting all those (whether feminists or sexists) who see Yahweh as a male deity. "God is neither male nor female," she claims, "and yet detecting divine transcendence in human reality requires human clues. Unique among them . . . is sexuality . . . To describe male and female, then, is to perceive the image of God; to perceive the image of God is to glimpse the transcendence of God . . . In this metaphor the vehicle contributes explicit meanings, while the tenor exists through hints and guesses" (pp. 21–22).

Trible unjustly restricts the rhetorical function of Genesis 1:27. This parallelism could be perceived as a literal analogy between the human and divine realms. It could also be construed as a metonymy: "male and female" being extensions or contiguous aspects of the "image of God." Furthermore, even if this verse is perceived as a metaphor, why must God be the tenor? Genesis 1:27 is primarily a poetic celebration of the special status of humanity as the climax of creation. God is not quite the topic.

Using this metaphor as an interpretive clue, Trible goes on to suggest that the imagery of God needs to be analyzed in light of both the feminine and masculine facets of the divine image. But already in the final line of this introductory chapter, Genesis 1:27 turns into "a metaphor that highlights *female* imagery for God" (p. 23; emphasis added). Similarly, Trible's discussion throughout *God and the Rhetoric of Sexuality* focuses on female metaphors for God (God as mother, midwife, mistress). The predominant male metaphors (God as father, husband, warrior) remain unexamined.

But let us now consider Trible's detailed analysis of Genesis 2–3. Unlike Stanton, she does not reject the second account, nor does she see it as a less refined sexist text which contradicts the egalitarian depiction of creation in Genesis 1. Trible neglects to take into account the differences between the Yahwistic text and the Priestly one, or, rather, she ignores the findings of historical biblical criticism. This is but one example of the anachronism which her ahistorical New Critical approach involves.[7] Seeking an organic unity of the text, she ignores the poetic and political implications of the stitching together of diverse documents dating from different periods.

Trible begins her chapter on Genesis 2–3 with a list of traditional interpretations which she refutes one by one. She refutes, for example, the common notion that God created man first and shows that even if this were the case, it does not necessarily imply his superiority vis-à-vis woman. Relying on the fact that *ha'adam* is a generic Hebrew term meaning "humankind," she suggests that it is not man who is created in 2:7, but a sexually undifferentiated "earth creature." (Trible thus underscores the biblical pun which links the terms *ha'adam* [humankind] and *'adama* [earth]). Human sexuality is created only in 2:22–23. Only after God

> operates on this earth creature, to produce a companion, its identity becomes sexual. The surgery is radical, for it results in two creatures where before there was only one. The new creature, built from the material of *ha-adam,* is female, receiving her identity in a word that is altogether new to the story, the word *'išša.* The old creature transformed is male, similarly receiving identity in a word that is new in the story, *'iš* . . . In the very act of distinguishing female from male, the earth creature describes her as "bone of my bones and flesh of my flesh" (2:23). These words speak unity, solidarity, mutuality, and equality. Accordingly, in this poem the man does not depict himself as either prior to or superior to the woman. His sexual identity depends upon her even as hers depends upon him.   (pp. 98–99)

Trible's insistence on the ambiguity of the term *ha'adam* in the story as well as her suggestion that sexual differentiation takes place only when the concepts *'ish* and *'ishsha* are created are most convincing. Her argument, however, becomes murky once the earth creature is transformed into a male creature, or rather when the term *ha'adam* is still used after sexual differentiation takes place as the proper name of the first man. In other words, instead of dealing with the ongoing fluidity and built-in ambiguity of the term *ha'adam* and examining its possible functions, she attributes one meaning exclusively to 2:7–21 and the other to 2:22–23.

It is fascinating to see how the same details can be read so differently by different feminists. When dealing with the material from which woman was created, Trible, unlike de Beauvoir, sees God's building *(bnh)* of woman from the rib as a sign of her uniqueness not only vis-à-vis man but also with respect to the rest of creation. (Trible rightly points out that, in addition to the earth creature, animals and plants were also created from earth.) After depicting the complex mysterious work which the creation of woman involved, she concludes that "woman is no weak, dainty, ephemeral creature. No opposite sex, no second sex, no derived sex—in short, no 'Adam's rib.' Instead, woman is the culmination of creation, fulfilling humanity in sexuality. Equal in creation with the man, she is, at this point [Genesis 2:23] elevated in emphasis by the design of the story" (p. 102).

In Trible's hands the Bible almost turns into a feminist manifesto, where every detail suspiciously ends up supporting woman's liberation. This is also the case with her treatment of the Fall. When dealing with the conversation of woman and serpent, she describes the first woman as an intelligent, perceptive, informed theologian or exegete who, unlike her passive partner, is familiar with the divine command and doesn't hesitate to reflect on it. Woman's decision to eat of the fruit of knowledge is accordingly seen as a courageous act which above all reflects her quest for knowledge. Only when Trible discusses the respective punishments of man and woman does she speak of the strife between the sexes and the inequality brought about by their transgression. But here too equality is somehow maintained, for "woman is corrupted in becoming a slave, and the man is corrupted in becoming the master" (p. 128). Moreover, the God responsible for the formation of these sex roles remains immaculate. Yahweh, according to Trible, does not prescribe such sex roles but rather presents them as the bleak result of transgression. "This statement [that the husband rule over his wife] is not license for male supremacy, but rather it is condemnation of that very pattern. Subjugation and supremacy are perversions of creation" (1976:20).

Esther Fuchs

In the mid-eighties a few comprehensive feminist critiques outside the domain of religious studies emerged, in part, I would suggest, in response to the flourishing of the literary approach to the Bible,[8] and in part as a result of the regenerated interest in male texts. Two articles by Esther Fuchs on the characterization of women in the Bible appeared in 1985. These were followed by an article concerning the patriarchal functions of biblical type-scenes in 1987 and an article on Rachel's story in 1988. Fuchs's main objective is to examine the political implications of supposedly "innocuous poetic constructions." Following the preliminary guidelines set in the writings of de Beauvoir, and especially in those of Millett, she focuses on the repressive androcentric aspects of biblical poetics, offering "a theoretical articulation of biblical sexual politics, or the ways by which the biblical narrative universalizes and legislates its male centered epistemology" (1986).

Fuchs, however, does not provide an extensive analysis of the creation of woman. She rightly asserts that the victimization of woman in Genesis 2–3 has been acknowledged by numerous feminist critics, suggesting that what is still lacking is a comprehensive literary critical study of the Hebrew Bible as a whole. Nevertheless, in "Who is Hiding the Truth? Deceptive Women and Biblcal Androcentrism," Fuchs briefly analyzes Eve as the prototypical deceptive woman. "Deceptiveness is a common characteristic of women in the Hebrew Bible," she claims "From Eve to Esther, from Rebekah to Ruth, the characterization of women presents deceptiveness as an almost inescapable feature of femininity" (1985:137).

She goes on to suggest that Eve is an exemplary case of

how the characterization of woman as deceptive "perpetuates the subordination of women based on their alleged moral deficiency" (p. 143). Yet if one reads Genesis closely, it becomes clear that Eve does not deceive (see Bal 1987). She simply gives the fruit to her partner (no dialogue is recorded), and he eats it.

In a later article, "For I Have the Way of Women" (1988), Fuchs finally admits that men too are occasionally presented as tricksters in the Bible; but then she hastens to rely on clear-cut oppositions, according to which the male protagonists remain the "good guys," despite their acts of deception, while the female characters are doomed by their nature to be eternally "bad."

Fuchs's criticism of Trible, Daly, and others can be applied to her own treatment of the Bible. Her analysis of biblical texts is rigidly selective and univocal. Fuchs's most important contribution is her insistence upon the importance of the underlying patriarchal assumptions of biblical poetics. Her analyses, however, fail to address the complexity of biblical texts.

Mieke Bal

Mieke Bal's *Lethal Love* (1987)—followed by *Murder and Difference* (1988a), and *Death and Dissymmetry* (1988b)—is to my mind a groundbreaking comprehensive feminist critique of the Hebrew Bible. Combining literary theory, feminism, semiotics, and psychoanalysis, Bal offers a refreshingly intricate approach to the Bible, and in this respect she is a fine representative of the more theoretically sophisticated third wave of feminist criticism. For Bal, the Bible is neither "a feminist resource" nor "a sexist manifesto." Such an assumption, she believes, "can be an issue only for those who attribute moral, religious, or political authority to these texts, which is precisely the opposite of what I am interested in" (1987:1).

Accordingly, she does not set out, as Trible does, to "restore" an "original" or privileged meaning of the Bible; instead she attempts to provide a "different" reading that would highlight "the relative arbitrariness of all readings, including the sexist readings we have become so used to" (p. 2). Bal's alternative readings are meant to serve as a critique of the misogynist monolithic stance that most interpretations of the Bible share despite their diversity. To illustrate this point, she discusses different types of reception—from literary scholarship to children's Bibles—in her analysis of five biblical love stories. What Bal attempts to show in each case is how the heterogeneous ideology of the text is turned into a monolithic one in the respective patriarchal interpretations she criticizes. How is this different from Trible's depatriarchalization of biblical interpretation? First, unlike Trible, Bal engages in an extensive semiotic analysis of the interpretations she refers to, laying bare the reading strategies at work. Second, her perception of misogyny, unlike the more traditional definition of Trible, is informed by deconstruction. What bothers Bal "is not the sexist interpretation of the Bible as such . . . It is the possibility of dominance itself, the attractiveness of coherence and authority in culture, that I see as the source rather than the consequence, of sexism" (p. 3). With such a definition of sexism, Trible's work, "in spite of its feminist intentions," becomes but another example of a reading that "does not escape the dominance of male interests."

While I tend to agree with Bal's criticism of Trible's work, I find her definition of a feminist reading of the Bible restrictive insofar as it presupposes that feminism is synonymous with modernity. In keeping with the writings of Derrida and Lacan, Bal defines the feminine as that which

exceeds the comprehension of the Cartesian subject, that
which is nontruth, nondecidability and nonknowledge. Yet,
while other feminist theorists, notably Luce Irigaray, Julia
Kristeva, and Hélène Cixous, have used modernist discourse
and its feminization of difference with some reservations and
modifications, in Bal's work the French masters are accepted
uncritically.

In focusing on Bal's "Sexuality, Sin, and Sorrow" (the
title of the chapter that deals with the love story of Adam and
Eve), I will do some injustice to the purposefully heterogeneous character of her work. Her treatment of the story of
Samson and Delilah, where the hermeneutic framework is
psychoanalytic and the type of reception is children's Bibles,
surely differs from her analysis of Genesis 1–3, where the hermeneutic framework is formalist and the type of reception is
Christian mythology. Nevertheless, there is enough of the
same in Bal's work to make "Sexuality, Sin, and Sorrow"
representative of her approach.

Bal sets out to provide a linear reading of Genesis 1–3.
Linearity is possible, she claims, since the two accounts of
creation are not contradictory, as some critics would have it.
The authors of the Priestly document were "good readers,"
who developed the conception of "creation through differentiation" evident in the older Yahwistic text (p. 119). And
yet what Bal actually provides is not a linear analysis of
Genesis 1–3 but a detailed reading of Genesis 2–3, with sporadic references to Genesis 1 at points in which the first
account corroborates her hypotheses.

Bal's focus on the second account has to do with the fact
that the type of reception she attempts to deconstruct in this
case is Paul's notorious reading of Genesis 2–3: "Let the
woman learn in silence with all subjection. But I suffer not a
woman to teach, nor to usurp authority over the man, but to
be in silence. For Adam was first formed, then Eve. And
Adam was not deceived, but the woman being deceived was

in the transgression. Notwithstanding she shall be saved in childbearing" (1 Tim. 2:11–15). Refuting such misogynist assumptions, however, is not the sole objective of Bal's analysis. It is also meant to serve as a critique of the formalist definition(s) of character, primarily those according to which a character is either a performer of action (an actant), a conglomeration of traits, or a combination of both. While acknowledging the value of such definitions—especially Shlomith Rimmon-Kenan's observations concerning the interdependence of "doing" (action) and "being" (features)— Bal points to two problems inherent in all formalist approaches to character. First, they neglect to consider the ideological implications of characters; and second, they neglect semiotic chronology. That is, such definitions fail to consider characters as products of "textual development," falsely assuming that characters "exist from the first time they are mentioned until the end" (p. 107).

By the end of the theoretical introduction to this chapter Paul seems to share some of the mistaken assumptions of the formalists. In his reading of Genesis 2–3 he relies on what Bal calls the "retrospective fallacy," a fallacy that "consists of the projection of an accomplished and singular named character onto previous textual elements that lead to the construction of that character" (p. 108). The proper name "Eve," she claims, appears only in the end of Genesis 3; "what existed before was an earth creature, then a woman, next an actant, then a mother, and, finally a being named 'Eve.'" Starting at the end, Paul lost sight of the gradual formation of the female character.

But let us follow, step by step, Bal's analysis of the construction of character by the Yahwist(s). In the beginning, says Bal (following Trible), "a sexless creature is formed. The first body, *the* body, unique and undivided, is the body of the earth creature, the work of Yahweh the potter. From 2:7 to 2:20 this creature has no name, no sex, and no activity. It emerges as a character-to-be" (pp. 112–113). After the emergence of the human body, sexual differentiation takes place. From a semiotic point of view (contra Paul), it is the woman who is formed first, then man; it is *ishsha* (female) who changes the meaning of *ha'adam* from earth creature to earth-man. Although man is the first to speak and differentiate, the woman is the first to be differentiated. The result is what Bal calls an "equalizing dialectic": man and woman mutually constitute each other, and in this respect they are created at the same time. The second creation story thus turns out to be "a specified narration of what events are included in the idea that 'God created them male and female'" (p. 119). The notion that the Priestly text is "the equal rights" version and the Yahwistic text is the "sexist" account is refuted. For Bal, both stories portray a simultaneous creation of male and female.

The next step is the emergence of activity, another crucial factor in the formation of character. The possibility of action is introduced by the serpent. Woman and serpent are primarily "generalizations of species or sex . . . but the confrontation brings them a step closer to the status of character" (p. 120). When woman finally chooses to disobey and eats from the fruit of the tree of knowledge, she performs the first independent act, promoting her status in the narrative. The feature this act entails for the woman (and eventually for her mate) is wisdom (and here Bal relies on Rimmon-Kenan's notion of the interdependence of "doing" and "being"). Wisdom, in this case, means having the ability to accept the human condition—namely, sexuality and death—being realistic, opting for the species' immortality instead of an impossible individual mode of immortality. In Bal's reading of Genesis the woman's disobedient act is anything but deceptive (once again, contra Paul). Eating from the forbidden fruit is regarded as an attempt to see beyond "false appearances," to "open one's eyes."

The final step is the emergence of the proper name. This step becomes possible only after God, in response to human transgression, endows man and woman with definite and restrictive features, when Yahweh creates sexual roles: man/ breadwinner/master vs. woman/mother/subordinate. The "empty," purely relational, terms *'ish* and *'ishsha* are replaced by a definition of sexual difference which has ideological implications. Accordingly, for Bal, the sexist ideology of the text begins at this point and not prior to it (p. 128). When the proper name finally emerges, it seals and reinforces the definition of woman's social role. The name "Eve," which is interpreted by Adam to mean "the mother of all living," imprisons the first woman in motherhood. "Eve, Mary's presumably negative counterpart, had in fact a better start, representing both sexuality and motherhood. The man, however, fails to appreciate that: after his celebration of love [in Gen. 2:23–24], now forgotten, he exclusively stresses the other side of woman: motherhood" (p. 128). Paul, who started at the end, at the proper name, projected Eve's later status onto the creation of the female body, drawing the false conclusion that woman was a secondary creation, subordinate to man from the very beginning.

In many ways the respective interpretations of Trible and Bal are similar. Both support the notion of an egalitarian creation of man and woman out of a sexually undifferentiated earth creature; both emphasize the first woman's wisdom; and both see 3:16 as the first point in which a sexist ideology is inscribed in the text. What makes their readings different is not only their distinct theoretical approaches and interests but also their respective treatment of Yahweh. Even when Bal, like Trible, finds equality at points that may seem inappropriate (such as Gen. 2:23), her objective is not to vindicate God. In Bal's reading of Genesis, Yahweh's status is not overrated, nor is he exempt from literary examination. To be more specific, his development as a character is presented as

analogous to that of the first human pair. If man and woman
are formed through mutual semiotic structuring, so is God.
It is the confrontation with woman and man which turns "the
almighty God of Genesis 1 into a character of equal status,
equal features, equal feelings to the others. From now on this
creating Spirit (Gen. 1:2) has a body; one that seeks the fresh-
ness in the garden, strolls in it and looks for its fellow inhabitants; he has a personality that makes him angry and even
later (Gen. 3:22), afraid" (p. 125).

I find Bal's sensitive discussion of the various phases of
the development of character intriguing, but her analysis
raises a few questions. To begin with her critique of Paul's
"retrospective fallacy," one may well ask whether Paul's retrospective restructuring of the story needs to be seen as a fallacy. Isn't it an inevitable part of the process of reading, as
Iser and other reader-response critics have amply shown? And
if this is a fallacy, is not Bal's reading of Genesis 2–3 in light
of Genesis 1 an "anticipatory fallacy?" I would find Bal's
argument far more convincing had she analyzed Paul's reading strategies without implying that such a retrospective
move is necessarily false or sexist. As for her emphasis on the
proper name as the point in which the character fully
emerges, this too may be questioned in light of the very
assumptions Bal initially relies on. If, as she argues in the theoretical introduction to this chapter, the proper name is that
which "provides the illusion of fullness," why does she accept
this illusion in her own analysis? Why does she see the emergence of the proper name as the final step? Shouldn't Eve's
role as a name-giver in Genesis 4 be considered another
important phase that somewhat undermines God's definition
of the sexual roles in Genesis 3:16–19? Finally, isn't Bal's suggestion that the name "Eve" initiates a split between sexuality
and motherhood, which culminates in the representation of
Mary, an imposition of a Christian concept on the biblical
text? Sexuality and motherhood go hand in hand for Eve in

4:1. Similarly, Adam's celebration of sexuality in 2:23 (which he supposedly forgets once he restricts Eve to motherhood) is at the same time a curious celebration of procreation, as I will attempt to show in Chapter 3.

The Book of J

I have chosen to discuss *The Book of J* (1990) by Harold Bloom, not because it forms part of feminist biblical criticism (although this is a fairly common notion), but rather because it has stimulated much interest in gender issues in the Bible. The sensational proposal that turned Bloom's book into a best-seller is that J, contrary to what biblical scholars usually assume, was not a male author (or a group of male authors), but a woman writer, whose sublime and sophisticated work has been continuously misread by normative tradition. Bloom even ventures to provide J with a definite location in time and place. She presumably lived during the reign of King Rehoboam of Judah, Solomon's son, and was affiliated with his court.

It is Bloom's fascination with the idea that part of the Bible was written by a woman and his pronounced admiration for his female J that have given rise to the assumption that his work must be compelling from a feminist perspective. There may indeed be something seductive about envisioning a past in which a woman had a central cultural position, yet one must bear in mind that Bloom's proposal is problematic, not only because of its highly speculative character and its anachronistic perception of authorship (this ancient document more likely represents the work of a school rather than a single author) but also because of its unmistakable patriarchal inclinations.[9]

Bloom's discovery of a "strong" female author at the very foundation of the Bible (the Yahwistic strand is supposedly the earliest) calls to mind the work of the nineteenth-

century scholar J. J. Bachofen, who discovered a matriarchal era
at the base of Western culture.[10] Both Bloom and Bachofen
are sincere in their admiration of female power in ancient
times; nonetheless, their romantic speculations concerning
the feminine roots of culture end up endorsing and venerating
male rule.

Adrienne Rich provides an insightful critique of Bachofen's depiction of matriarchy in *Of Woman Born* (1986:86–89).
She shows how Bachofen, despite his praise of maternal wisdom, treats the matriarchal age as an inferior phase bound up
with the world of matter. Bachofen regards matriarchal culture as an important improvement on the age that preceded
it: the tellurian (earth-derived) swamp life (characterized by
sexual promiscuity); yet he insists that the rule of the mothers
is but a stepping-stone toward the highest phase of all,
patriarchy, in which the spirit is wholly liberated from the
phenomena of natural life. Thus, Bachofen claims that "The
more savage the men of this first period, the more necessary
becomes the restraining force of women . . . Matriarchy is
necessary to the education of mankind and particularly of
men. Just as the child is first disciplined by his mother, so the
races of men are first disciplined by woman. The male must
serve before he can govern" (1967:143–144).

In the *Book of J* one finds a similar move. Bloom raves
about J's brilliance, yet he is far less interested in J than in
what he considers her greatest literary creation—the uncanny
and impish Yahweh, a God who has very little to do with the
transcendent perfect God theologians cherish. In fact, he
turns J into a typical Jewish mother (with all the patriarchal
implications of this stereotype), whose main purpose in life
is to raise Yahweh, her "genius" son. J's Yahweh, Bloom
writes, is "an imp who behaves sometimes as though he is
rebelling against his Jewish mother" (p. 15). But she, J,
knows how to handle him. Her "attitude toward Yahweh
resembles nothing so much as a mother's somewhat wary but

still proudly amused stance toward a favorite son" (p. 26). J,
like Bachofen's matriarchs, is presented as a wonderful nur-
turer who knows how to ensure the development of childish
male rascals.[11]

What, then, are the literary grounds which suddenly
convinced Bloom that J was a woman? Bloom doesn't really
provide a substantial explanation. He suggests that J's femininity is revealed in her preference of heroines to heroes. "I
think it accurate to observe that J had no heroes, only heroines. Sarai and Rachel are wholly admirable, and Tamar, in
proportion to the narrative space she occupies, is very much
the most vivid portrait in J. But Abram, Jacob, and Moses
receive a remarkably mixed treatment from J" (p. 32). Elsewhere, he similarly contends that "misogyny in the West is a
long and dismal history of weak misreadings of the comic J,
who exalts women throughout her work" (p. 178). Bloom
is right to worry about being accused of essentialism (see
p. 10). Sympathy for the plight of women is not gender-
bound and may be found in male works as well. *Anna
Karenina, Madame Bovary,* and *The Book of J* are proof of this.

What is even more disturbing about Bloom's claim is its
simplification of the intricate characterization evident in the
Yahwistic strand, and for that matter in the Hebrew Bible as
a whole. The biblical writers (whoever they may have been)
did not believe in "wholly admirable" characters. What they
offer—and this is one of the intriguing features of this text—
is a mixed treatment of all characters, regardless of gender or
nationality. Esau, represented as unfit to become the heir,
evokes much empathy when he weeps over his sad fate, just
as Jacob, father of the nation, does not escape criticism for
deceiving his elder brother. Similarly, female characters, even
though their status is officially inferior to that of male characters, are constructed according to the same poetic principle:
their brief histories consist of a mixture of twists and turns,
of admirable deeds and moments of weakness.

Let me stress that I share Bloom's fascination with the aesthetic intensity of the Yahwistic strand and agree that some of the most powerful women in the Pentateuch are indeed to be found in this textual layer. Yet in order to better understand the Yahwist(s)' perception of gender, one needs to pay close attention not only to the unconventional strength of Yahwistic female characters but also to the ways in which it is often repressed. Bloom, in other words, ignores the ideological heterogeneity of the Yahwistic strand. But then he says altogether very little about ideological matters. He regards J's work, like his own, as innocent of "tendentious purposes" (p. 10), beyond ideology and as such, beyond ideological critique.[12]

In magnifying the status of female characters in biblical texts, Bloom in a sense is a follower of Trible, whose work, however, is never mentioned in the book. In particular like Trible, Bloom views the creation of woman as the culmination of creation.

> But we should stand back here and contrast Yahweh as the artificer of the woman with Yahweh as the much more child-like and haphazard creator of the man. It is not just that J has given six times the space to woman's creation as to man's; it is the difference between making a mud pie and building a much more elaborate and fairer structure. The man provides (involuntarily) the substance with which Yahweh begins this second and greater creation . . . Surely J's ironic point is that the second time around, Yahweh has learned better how the job ought to be done. (1990:179–180)

There is, however, a significant difference. In contrast to Trible, Bloom focuses on the development of Yahweh as a young artist rather than on the characterization of Eve. Here as elsewhere, despite his provocative claims concerning their superior character, Bloom ends up devoting very little time to Yahwistic heroines.

It is certainly to Bloom's credit that he has succeeded in shaking his readers out of their preconceptions about the Bible—both in emphasizing the impious literary ingenuity of the Yahwistic strand and in insisting on a different reading of J's gender—and yet his work offers but little insight into gender constructions in the Hebrew Bible.

Conclusion

Regardless of the striking diversity of the six feminist readings of the creation stories discussed, what they all share— from Elizabeth Cady Stanton's interpretation in *The Woman's Bible* to Mieke Bal's "Sexuality, Sin, and Sorrow"—is an ideological critique of patriarchy. Even when the patriarchal bias of the Bible is not extensively tackled, as in Trible's work, the point of departure is nonetheless critical. Patriarchy is challenged.

By sketching the history of feminist biblical criticism— a history which as yet has not received the attention it deserves from biblical scholars and literary critics—I have tried to show that this is a dynamic and fruitful critical field whose contribution to the understanding of the Bible and of the social dimension of literary power in general is most significant. The Bible is a text whose narrative is considered as Law, as *binding;* and as such it is a remarkable example of how literature cannot be dissociated from ideology. If Paul can use the story of Eve's creation to validate his resolution that woman should not be allowed to teach, nor "to usurp authority over man," it is precisely because the Bible has accumulated tremendous social force over the many centuries in which it has been read and reread.

How the Bible has acquired such force and to what extent its social use has been compatible with the ideology initially encoded within it are questions to which different feminists, as we have seen, provide different answers. In keeping with Mieke Bal's argument, I do not believe in the possibility of uncovering the "original" biblical stance on gender issues. Yet if we attempt to explore the *historical* context in which biblical texts were first formed and circulated, we will, I think, come closer to comprehending both their past and present influence on the ways sexual differentiation is created.

ⲻ ⲻ 3 ⲻ

Beyond Genesis 3: The Politics
of Maternal Naming

No feminist critic of the Bible has neglected to discuss the
story (or stories) of the creation of woman; and yet, despite
significant differences in theoretical approach and focus, their
readings generally have been confined to Genesis 1–3. One
may well ask why. Both J and P develop their respective perceptions of femininity vis-à-vis creation beyond Genesis 3 as
well. Genesis 1–3 may in fact be construed as part of a larger
unit, what historical-critical scholarship has called "primeval
history," which ends only at Genesis 11, where the history of
the patriarchs and matriarchs commences. This textual unit
consists of a *series* of narratives and genealogies dealing with
creation, crime and punishment, or both.

The tendency to focus on Genesis 1–3 (common not
only among feminists) derives in part from the continuing
impact of the Christian perception of the Fall as the unequiv-
ocal conclusion of Creation (see Westermann 1972:2–3).
There is, however, no concept of an Original Fall in Genesis.
Primeval characters fall time and again in a variety of ways.
The first fall is not singled out. Fratricide, sleeping with the
Sons of God, incest, and the building of the Tower of Babel
are transgressions as exemplary as the eating of the forbidden
fruit. Similarly, creation is an ongoing process. The world is

wholly destroyed and recreated in the story of the Flood; and on a less cosmic level, this is true of most stories in this unit.

Many feminist critics have sharply critiqued Christian interpretations of the creation stories, but they have done so without calling into question the status of the Fall as a conclusive boundary. Elizabeth Cady Stanton (1895), Kate Millett (1969), Mary Daly (1973), Phyllis Trible (1978), and Mieke Bal (1987) provocatively turn the story of man's Fall through woman (as in Paul's reading) into the story of woman's Fall through man, ignoring the fact that Eve does not vanish after Genesis 3, nor does she hesitate to rise and fall once again in Genesis 4.

I will show that the analysis of Genesis 4–11, and especially of Genesis 4–5, is essential to an understanding of both the Priestly and Yahwistic treatments of femininity in Genesis 1–3. I begin with J's immediate continuation of the story of the Garden of Eden. In the opening verses of Genesis 4 we learn that Adam and Eve, after their banishment, make use of the "knowledge" they acquired back west in the Garden. As a result two sons are born, and Genesis 2–3 is linked to the story of Cain and Abel. Knowledge, especially in its sexual sense, is no longer an abstract notion. Now that it is within human reach, propagation takes place and a new mode of discourse arises: genealogy.[1]

Maternal Naming-Speeches

What interests me most about this genealogical note is the point in Genesis 4:1 where Eve, who previously was an object of naming, becomes a subject of naming. At the birth of her first son the primordial mother delivers a fascinating naming-speech: *qaniti 'ish 'et YHWH* (rendered by Cassuto as "I have created a man [equally/together] with the Lord" [1961: 198])—setting the ground for maternal naming-speeches in the Bible.

Naming is not only Adam's prerogative, as Mary Daly (1973:8) claims, nor is it necessarily a paternal medium. Eve is no exception; more often than not it is the *mother* (or surrogate mother) who names the child.[2] My intention is not to reverse Daly's observations—the very fact that biblical mothers name only their sons and not their daughters (with the exception of Dinah) indicates that their power of naming is limited by patriarchal exigencies—but rather to point to the complexity of the interrelations of power and naming in Genesis. Eve is both the object and the subject of naming; and it is her latter capacity that is particularly characteristic of women in the Bible.

Contra Mieke Bal, the one feminist critic with whom I will engage in a more extensive dialogue, I would argue that Eve's impressive comeback as a name-giver in Genesis 4— and not the emergence of the proper name "Eve"—is the final stroke in the formation of the first female character. In an intriguing analysis of phases in the textual development of the first woman, Bal perceives Adam's naming of Eve as the conclusive step that marks the Fall of woman and seals her sexual and social role (as defined in Gen. 3:16). In choosing to call her *Hawwa,* a name he interprets as "the mother of all living" (Gen. 3:20), Adam, according to Bal, determines her character: Eve, from now on, "is imprisoned in motherhood" (1987:128).[3] But Bal both mystifies the power of proper names and exaggerates the restrictive nature of Eve's motherhood. Above all, her adherence to the traditional Christian delimitation of the creation stories prevents her from considering the continuation of the representation of the first woman in Genesis 4. She thus overlooks an important means of characterization for women in the Bible, and especially in Genesis: naming-speeches. One should bear in mind that biblical naming (especially when accompanied by a speech) usually reveals more about the character of the name-giver than the recipient (see Sternberg 1985:330–331). The sequence of

speeches of Leah and Rachel wonderfully illustrates this phenomenon in its encapsulation of the sisters' rivalry, of their
respective relations to Jacob and to God, and their joy at the
birth of their sons.

> And Leah conceived, and bare a son, and she called his name
> Reuben: for she said, Surely the Lord hath looked [*ra'a*] upon
> my affliction; now therefore my husband will love me. And
> she conceived again, and bare a son; and said, Because the Lord
> hath heard [*shama'*] that I was hated, he hath therefore given
> me this son also: and she called his name Simeon [*Shim'on*] . . .
> And Bilhah conceived, and bare Jacob a son. And Rachel said,
> God hath judged [*danani*] me, and hath also heard my voice,
> and hath given me a son: therefore called she his name Dan.
> And Bilhah Rachel's maid conceived again, and bare Jacob a
> second son. And Rachel said, With great wrestlings have I
> wrestled [*niftalti*] with my sister, and I have prevailed: and she
> called his name Naphtali . . . And God remembered Rachel,
> and God hearkened to her, and opened her womb. And she
> conceived, and bare a son; and said, God hath taken away my
> reproach: And she called his name Joseph [*Yosef*]; and said,
> The Lord shall add [*yosef*] to me another son.   (Gen. 29:32–
> 30:24)[4]

Eve's speech at first may seem more a drawn shutter than
a window; yet, not unlike the speeches of Rachel and Leah, it
functions as a means of characterization. Genesis 4:1 presents
another phase in the formation of the first woman's relation to
God and Adam as it offers a glimpse of her own perception of
motherhood and (pro)creation. (In Genesis 3 Eve's maternal
role is seen only through the eyes of God and Adam.)

Before analyzing the first maternal speech to be delivered, a preliminary note on this means of characterization is
necessary. Among the various devices of characterization in
biblical narrative, direct speech predominates. Robert Alter
suggests that the preference for direct discourse is compatible
with the monotheistic perception of human freedom. The

omniscient biblical narrator "does not openly meddle with the personages he presents" (1981:87); rather, he allows them to speak for themselves, with minimal authorial intrusion, giving them enough rope to do as they please.

Naming-speeches are a special type of direct speech, hovering between interior speech and a vocalized ceremonial discourse. (The ambiguity of the biblical "said," between thought and speech, confirms this fluidity.[5]) They are constructed, with some variations, according to the following formula: s/he named the child's name X; for s/he said . . . (the explanation for the name).[6] Although at times the word "for" *(ki; 'al-ken)* or one of two verbs, "named" *(vayikra/vatikra)* or "said" *(vayomer/vatomer),* are missing, the speech always consists of a pun which creates a phonetic link between the name and its interpretation.[7] Eve's speech thus follows the formal conventions of biblical naming-speeches; it links the name "Cain" *(Qayin)* and the verb *qana* (create) by means of a pun. This phonetic association does not imply that there is an etymological affinity between the two words. "Cain" in fact derives from the root *qyn* (not *qnh*), meaning "to shape," or "fashion" in the context of metal-working. In 4:1 a semantic link is at work (*qyn* is a segment which pertains to the semantic field of "creation"), but this is rarely the case. As Speiser puts it, "a correct or even plausible linguistic derivation would be purely coincidental [in naming-speeches], since the play on the name was the significant thing—aetiology rather than etymology" (1964:232).[8]

Uprising

Turning to the thematic level, one may well ask: But what does *qaniti 'ish 'et YHWH* mean? Although most commentators would agree that, generally speaking, this speech expresses the primordial mother's joy at the birth of Cain, their translations and interpretations differ significantly. This

is far from surprising: every word in this speech poses a problem. The verb *qana* is polysemic, a feature which has allowed
the by-now-discredited translation "to acquire" instead of the
less theologically palatable "to create" (see Westermann
1972:290). The use of the word *'ish* (man) for a newborn boy
is odd. But the final part *'et YHWH* (literally, with the Lord)
has been by far the most perplexing element. God of course
is always present in procreation—opening wombs, giving
seed. What is more, He is often an implied addressee in naming-speeches, as is evident in Genesis 29–30. But in Genesis
4:1, He is treated scandalously as a partner, not quite as the
pivot around whom everything swerves. Most translations
(for example, the King James: "I have gotten a man from the
Lord"; the old JPS [Jewish Publication Society]: "I have
acquired a man with the help of God"; the new JPS: "I have
gained a male child with the help of the Lord") mitigate the
problematic aspects of the verse, which is why I rely on
Cassuto's rendition of this speech.

   Let us now follow Cassuto's interpretation of Genesis
4:1. "The first woman," he claims, "in her joy at giving birth
to her first son, boasts of her generative power, which
approximates in her estimation to the Divine creative power.
The Lord formed the first *man* (ii 7), and I have formed the
second *man . . . I stand together (i.e. equally) WITH HIM in
the rank of creators*" (1961:201). Note that for Cassuto *'et
YHWH* means not only "equally with" but also "together
with." Eve's position in the rank of creators allows her to
become God's partner in the work of creation; it allows her
to "feel the personal nearness of the Divine presence to herself" (p. 202).

   Cassuto supports his argument by showing that the verb
qnh in the sense of "create" is used both in reference to God's
creation of the world—as in the well-known expression *qone
shamayim va'arets,* "the maker of heaven and earth" (Gen.
14:22)—and, even more relevantly, in the context of divine

parental procreation. The two verses Cassuto quotes are: Psalms 139:13, "For Thou didst form [*qanita*] my inward parts, Thou didst knit me together in my mother's womb"; and Proverbs 8:22, The Lord created me [*qanani*] at the beginning of His way, the first of His acts of old. It is precisely by using a verb which in all other cases defines divine (pro)creation that Eve sets the birth of her son on the same footing with the birth of the race.

While some commentators have contested the meaning "create" for Genesis 4:1 because of its association with the divine realm, Cassuto, with his admirable sensitivity to the traces of pagan elements in the Hebrew Bible, avoids banalizing this speech. He goes on to present a Ugaritic parallel in which the same root (*qny* or *qnw*) appears in the title of Ashera, the Ugaritic mother goddess: *qnyt 'ilm,* "the creatress/bearer of the gods." The findings of John Skinner (1910:102–103) and, more recently, of Isaac Kikawada (1972:33–37) concerning this verse reinforce the notion that Eve is endowed with traits which in pagan works characterized the creatress. Skinner points to a strikingly similar verse in the the bilingual Babylonian creation myth: "Aruru [the mother goddess] together with him [Marduk] created the seed of mankind." Similarly, in the Atra-Hasis, as Kikawada points out, the creatress Mami (quite an appropriate name for a mother goddess) shapes a man out of clay with Enki's help. In both cases the word *itti,* meaning "with" or "together with" (analogous to the prepositional sense of the Hebrew *'et*), appears.

Eve's naming-speech may be perceived as a trace from an earlier mythological phase in which mother goddesses were very much involved in the process of creation, even if in a secondary position, under the auspices of the supreme male deity. What makes Cassuto's reading especially interesting is his consideration of the impact of this trace in the Bible. A speech of this sort cannot but be a bold provocation in a monotheistic context. If a mother goddess—be it Ashera, Aruru, or Mami—had delivered a similar speech, it could have been construed as "factual" or even as a token of modesty, but when the primordial biblical mother, who is a mere human being, claims to have generative powers which are not unlike God's, she is as far from modesty as one can get.[9]

Eve's hubristic tendencies do not begin here. Already in Genesis 3 the first woman violates the divine decree, opting to become like God. "Ye shall not surely die: For God doth know that in the day ye eat thereof, then your eyes shall be opened, and ye shall be as gods, knowing good and evil" (Gen. 3:4–5), says the serpent, and Eve, who finds his argument attractive, decides to rebel against God's possessive hold on knowledge. In fact, Eve's naming-speech is an interesting development of her first rebellion against the Father. If in Genesis 3 she sought to acquire a potential, in Genesis 4 the primordial mother explores the ways in which the knowledge she illegally acquired in the Garden of Eden may be realized. Her hubris is transferred to the realm of creativity. By defining herself as a creatress, she now calls into question the preliminary biblical tenet with respect to (pro)creation—God's position as the one and only Creator.

Hubris is not only characteristic of Eve in primeval history. Most primeval characters exceed human limits in one way or another. They all tend to be more theomorphic than postdiluvian characters. Enoch and Noah "walk with God" (another case of a provocatively intimate *'et,* meaning "with," vis-à-vis the Father); the Daughters of Adam sleep with the Sons of God; the people of Babel seek "to make a name for themselves" by building a Tower that would reach Heaven— and most of them enjoy a remarkable longevity, which seems a curious compromise between mortality and immortality. (It is only after the generation of the *nefilim,* the giants, that God decides to limit human longevity to one hundred twenty years at most.) What makes Eve's transgression of boundaries somewhat different is the fact that her speech is a critique not only of monotheistic principles but also of the underlying patriarchal presuppositions of monotheism. Unlike the inhabitants of Babel with their scandalous phallic creation, the first woman challenges *both* the divine restrictions on human creativity and the exclusion of the feminine from the representation of creation.

Reversal: Dialogic Naming

Eve's provocative speech is more than an expression of feminine pride directed toward God. Adam is another important addressee. The first woman, after all, is a servant of two masters. Here, as before, her conflict with God is inseparable from her relationship with Adam. Although in Genesis 3 Adam joins forces with Eve against the Master of Masters, the fact that she is punished for this conspiracy by subjugation to her accomplice suggests that these two male authorities have more in common than is apparent at first. How does Adam enter into the picture? Through the word *'ish.* Cassuto sees the unusual use of the term in this context as an evocation of God's creation of man in 2:7; but bearing in mind that the word *'adam* (and not *'ish*) is used in 2:7, one is led to look elsewhere. *'Ish,* I believe, primarily refers back to Adam's first naming-speech in 2:23—"This is now bone of my bones, and flesh of my flesh: she shall be called Woman [*'isha*], because she was taken out of Man [*'ish*]"—where the concept "man" first appears.

"The old naming was not a product of a dialogue—a fact inadvertently admitted in the Genesis story of Adam's naming the animals and woman," Daly writes in *Beyond God the Father* (1973:8). But there is more of a dialogue "in the old naming" than she suspects. *Qaniti 'ish 'et YHWH* is, among other things, a response to Adam's naming of woman; it is a response to his almost dreamlike reversal of the order of things, to his indirect claim to have created woman out of his body, to his celebration of the generative capacity of his flesh and bones. She responds in the medium he chose to use: naming-speeches. It is not you who created woman out of man (with divine help), she seems to claim, but it is I who created you—'*ish*—together with Yahweh! Second person is avoided, but the dialogic thrust is unmistakable. The rivalry between the sexes, not unlike the rivalry between Leah and Rachel, is represented at this point through a compelling exchange (almost a match) of naming-speeches.

To return to '*ish,* the marker that made this intertextual interaction possible, I would suggest that it be seen as a condensation of Cain and Adam.[10] Having two referents, '*ish* allows Eve to take pride in her role in the birth of Cain, as well as retroactively to point to the first man as another product of her creativity. Through her naming of Cain, Eve rewrites Genesis 2 as a subversive comment on Adam's displacement of the generative power of the female body. Perhaps her speech is a condensation of two versets (Adam's speech in Gen. 2 is a parallelism), which run as follows: "I shaped a child [*yeled*] equally with Yahweh / I created a man [*ish*] together with God." The second verset is, as is often the case, an intensified repetition of the first verset.[11] This of course is only a conjecture. Whether or not an uncondensed form of Eve's naming-speech actually existed, this parallelism may illustrate why condensation is altogether necessary, or why the text is so nebulous. Both conjectured versets are scandalous, but the latter one is the more so. If in the first verset the primordial mother overrates her maternal capacities, in the second she dares to change history; she presents herself not only as Cain's mother, but also as the bearer of Adam and perhaps even as the ex-consort of Yahweh. The conflation of the two ideas, which obscures the latent meanings of Eve's speech, is precisely what enables their representation; it is a consequence of censorship and a means of avoiding it.[12]

Bal's claim that the name "Eve" imprisons the first woman in motherhood should by now seem rather anachronistic. I do not mean to deny patriarchy's use of the institution of motherhood to repress women, but instead to point to the special features of this particular story. What is most striking about Genesis 2–3 is the extent to which woman is *denied* her role as mother, as creatress, by both God and Adam. She is called the "mother of all living" only at the very end, after all things already have been created by God and the first man. Had Adam called her Eve in Genesis 2, approximately where *adam* begins more clearly to function as a proper name (perhaps as a continuation of 2:24), his (pro)creative dream would have been undermined. It would have been a little too odd if he were to call his daughter, so to speak, the "mother of all living" right after creating her. The deferred emergence of the proper name "Eve" may thus be seen as a narratological strategy that enables Adam to act out his parturient fantasies, as a compensation for his relatively minute share in procreation.

One more crucial point indicates that a reversal of sexual roles is at stake here: this is the only time in the Bible where a man names a newly born female and delivers a speech to celebrate the occasion![13] Adam's naming of woman, which has been taken to be representative of male dominion in language, thus turns out to be the exception to the rule; it is meant to single out and glorify the creation of the first woman, while allowing Adam to play the (m)other's part.

In defining woman's creation out of Adam's body as a reversal of sexual roles, I have followed the traditional psychoanalytic focus. Rank, Freud, and Roheim interpret this reversal in Genesis 2 as a disguise for "the well-known motif of mother-incest."[14] Fromm (1951:233–234) perceives it as a manifestation of pregnancy envy; and Dundes (1983:35–53) argues that Adam's usurpation of a maternal role is a case of *couvade*. (The term *couvade* designates "a widespread custom whereby fathers or men about to become fathers ritually went through the motions of confinement and childbirth.")

On the question of male fantasies I am probably closest to Fromm, although I would change his diachronic depiction of the relations between pregnancy envy and penis envy (he suggests that the former preceded) with a synchronic one. Echoing J. J. Bachofen's views of an evolutionary sequence from matriarchy to patriarchy, Fromm defines Adam's creation of Eve as a trace left from a matriarchal era, from a time when the role of the mother was in fact enviable. "In order to defeat the mother, the male must prove that he is not inferior, that he has the gift to produce" (p. 233), and this is exactly what Adam tries to do. According to Fromm, it is only after the Fall, when God ascribes to Eve a subordinate role with respect to her husband, that male domination is established. "Quite obviously this establishment of male domination points to a previous situation in which he did not rule" (p. 234).

Bachofen's observations, however, are speculative. There is no clear-cut proof that a matriarchal order ever existed. But this does not necessarily undermine the relevance of pregnancy envy to Genesis 2. As Bruno Bettelheim suggests, *each sex* "feels envy in regard to the sexual organs and functions of the other" (1962:10). Pregnancy envy is as common a phenomenon in patriarchal society as penis envy, even if the former is more easily sublimated or compensated for in such a cultural context. Despite his superior role, Adam cannot help admiring, in Karen Horney's terms, "this life-creating power of woman . . . And this is exactly the point where problems arise. For it is contrary to human nature to sustain appreciation without resentment toward capabilities that one does not possess" (1967:115).

I would like to emphasize that my reading diverges significantly from the traditional psychoanalytic stance in one crucial point: it takes into consideration Eve's subjectivity and independent narratological position.[15] In quest of what is lacking in him, Adam seeks to appropriate the (m)other. But Eve doesn't acquiesce in this appropriation. She is not the perfect Other, nor is she a (m)other devoid of subjecthood. First in the Garden of Eden, and then in her naming-speech, the primordial mother challenges the attempts of both God and Adam to be the sole subjects of procreation.

Falling Again

I do not mean to turn the Bible into a feminist manifesto, but rather to show that while the dominant thrust of the Bible is clearly patriarchal, patriarchy is continuously challenged by antithetical trends. That such a challenge in turn does not escape critique may be seen not only in the punishment of Eve in Genesis 3 but also in the change in tone evident in Eve's second naming-speech, which pertains to the Yahwistic genealogy at the end of Genesis 4. Genesis 4:1 isn't quite the final note in the characterization of the first woman. "And Adam knew his wife again; and she bare a son, and called his name Seth [*Shet*]: For God, said she, hath appointed [*shat*] me another seed instead of Abel, whom Cain slew" (4:25).

If Eve was the subject of the earlier speech, now God is the subject, the one who "grants" *(shat)* a seed. He is restored to His conventional role as the protagonist of procreation. In contrast to Eve's first naming-speech, which dramatically inaugurated maternal name-giving by associating female generativity with cosmic creation, her second speech seems a more subdued model; and as such it can be less obscure than the first. Is Eve more modest and careful at this point as a result of her first encounter with death? Does she take God's punitive abilities a little more seriously now that death is no longer an abstract concept? Once again Cassuto is insightful:

> This time Eve does not give voice to feelings of joy and pride such as she expressed when her eldest son was born. Her mood is one of mourning and sorrow for the family calamity, and her words are uttered meekly, with humility and modesty. On the first occasion, she gloried in her creative power and her collaboration with the Lord; this son she now regards purely as a gift vouchsafed to her by Heaven. In the former instance, she mentioned the name of the the Lord, the Tetragrammaton, which signifies the Godhead in His personal aspect and direct relationship to His creatures . . . now, in the hour of her mourning, it seems as if God is far removed from her, in the supernal heights of Heaven . . . as that transcendental Power denoted by the appellation Elohim.   (1944:245–246)

While I disagree with Cassuto's description of the speech as an expression of mourning—it is, after all, primarily a celebration of birth, even if toned down—I find his analysis of the change that takes place in Eve's relation to God most convincing. Whether or not one accepts Cassuto's reading of the respective meanings of YHWH and Elohim (which is in a sense a development of the rabbinical notion that YHWH represents God's mercy, while Elohim denotes the distant God of strict judgment), the first woman, at this point, no longer regards God as cocreator, but rather as *the* Creator. Her words now convey respect for the boundaries between the human and divine realms.[16]

Taking Cassuto's observations a step further, I propose that this fall between Eve's first and second naming-speeches be added to the long list of Yahwistic stories of pride/crime and punishment in primeval history. (The question of human transgression is a Yahwistic specialty. All stories of crime and punishment in this unit are Yahwistic, with the exception of the Flood story, which is a patchwork of J and P.) My contention is, in other words, that the tragedy which befalls Eve's sons is meant, among other things, as a retributive deflation of her hubris. The son who was the object of her (pro)creative pride turns out to be the destroyer of her creation. This by no means implies that the killing of Abel and the banishment of Cain are Eve's fault; rather it is an indication of the complex interweaving of these two Yahwistic texts.[17] Interestingly, not unlike other stories which pertain to this list (the Garden of Eden, Cain and Abel, and the Flood, for example), destruction is followed by re-creation. The punishment is followed by a certain reconciliation between God and the "sinner": the first woman receives another son and renders unto God what is His.

Eve's acknowledgment of God's power, however, does not entail an acceptance of Adam's rule. The primordial mother still treats procreation as if it were an outcome of a transaction between God and her alone. Such transactions are a common topic in maternal naming-speeches (see Gen. 30:24; 1 Sam. 1:20). In a sense they serve as a female counterpart to the long conversations men have with God concerning seed and stars.

Creative Hierarchies

The ongoing tense interplay between a dominant patriarchal discourse and various opposing undercurrents is analogous to the tension between, in Robert Alter's words, "the divine plan and the disorderly character of actual historical events . . . between God's will, His providential guidance, and human freedom" (1981:33). God may be the ultimate authority, yet he is continuously disobeyed. Similarly, man has been officially allotted the position of master over woman, but this does not imply necessarily that she accepts his authority. Adam is not the last man to have "hearkened" to a woman's "voice." By the same token, Eve never fully acknowledges Adam's rule, as her naming-speeches indicate. And even if she accepts divine authority in her second naming-speech, this does not mean that her daughters will refrain from calling God's authority into question. The official hierarchy God-man-woman is never a stable one in the Yahwistic corpus, and to a lesser degree this is true of biblical narrative as a whole. The capacity to transgress boundaries is one of the essential traits of the biblical character, whether male or female. The difference lies in the respective position of man and woman in this hierarchic structure.

In the realm of creation, the "official" hierarchy goes as follows: God is the Creator, Adam is the Son of God, and Eve is the Daughter of Adam (to evoke another primeval story). David Damrosch aptly describes the relation between God and Adam in this respect: "in creating Adam, God sought to make an earthly representative, like himself but subordinate; and this is just what Adam himself proves to need. The problem for God here is that Adam is so much like God that he shares the lack that God had felt, and where God desired an Adam, Adam desires an Eve" (1987:140). But the story of creation does not end with the desires of God and Adam. The problem for both male authorities is that Eve rebels against her role as a subordinate of a subordinate in a field in which the female body has such a prominent role. Through the naming of her sons, the primordial mother insists upon her own generative powers and attempts to dissociate motherhood from subordination. By taking pleasure in her creativity she attempts to undo God's punishment in Genesis 3:16, to misread God's linking of female procreation with sorrow and with subjugation to man.

Exceeding the restrictive border of Genesis 3 makes one thing clear: the first feminist reader of the creation story is none other than Eve herself.

When P Expands on Genesis 1

The Priestly writers also go beyond Genesis 3 in their treatment of creation, mostly through long, uniform, and systematized genealogies called *toledot* (begettings), the very trademark of this strand (see Westermann, 1972:12–18 and 347–357). The *toledot* of Adam in Genesis 5, the Priestly response to the unruly narrativized genealogical notes of the Yahwist(s) in Genesis 4, commences with a recapitulation of the creation of humanity in Genesis 1:

> This is the book of the generations of Adam. In the day that God created man, in the likeness of God made he him; Male and female created he them; and blessed them, and called their name Adam, in the day when they were created. And Adam lived an hundred and thirty years, and begat a son in his own likeness, after his image; and called his name Seth. And the days of Adam after he had begotten Seth were eight hundred years: and he begat sons and daughters: And all the days that Adam lived were nine hundred and thirty years: and he died. And Seth lived an hundred and five years, and begat Enos: And Seth lived after he begat Enos eight hundred and seven years, and begat sons and daughters: And all the days of Seth were nine hundred and twelve years: and he died.   (Gen. 5:1–8)

Westermann rightly argues that this genealogy shows that "the plan of God in creating human beings is spelling itself out . . . The imperative 'be fruitful and multiply and fill the earth' is being carried out in Genesis 5. The power of the blessing shows itself effective in the relentless rhythm and steady succession of generations which stretch out across time" (1972:348).

Once God's plan is spelled out, however, the patriarchal presuppositions of the Priestly narrative become clear. No mother (or wife) is mentioned; no daughter's name forms part of the list. Surely the participation of females in these

begettings is implied by the repetition of the verse "male and
female created he them" at the very opening of the chapter
and by the explicit definition of *'adam* as a generic name in
5:2. But procreation becomes primarily a male issue once the
generic term *'adam* in 5:1–2 turns into the proper name Adam
in 5:3, once the relentless listing of ancestors begins. From
this point on fathers (from Adam to Noah) are presented as
the primary agents of the divine blessing.

Going beyond Genesis 3 to examine the Priestly depiction of the realization of the divine plan thus is essential to
the understanding of Genesis 1:27. Even if God, according
to P, created man and woman simultaneously, this act, as
Genesis 5 makes clear, does not quite prescribe equality
between the sexes. The Priestly work may be acknowledging
a certain symmetry between male and female on the cosmic
level, but when dealing with the social realm, procreation
turns out to be the perpetuation of male seed in male seed.
Elizabeth Cady Stanton (1985:20–21) and Phyllis Trible
(1978:1–31), who put great emphasis on the liberating quali-
ties of this verse—for the former it is proof that the "masculine and feminine elements exactly equal and balance each
other" both in the human realm and in the godhead, and for
the latter it serves as a guiding metaphor in the process of
"depatriarchalizing" biblical texts—take it out of context by
neglecting to examine its reappearance and development in
Genesis 5.

P versus J

The analysis of Genesis 4 and 5 may also illuminate the interrelations between the respective treatments of femininity in
the Yahwistic and Priestly texts. Unlike Bal, I do not find the
Priestly writers to be such "good readers" of their precur-
sor(s). In fact there is a good deal of misreading in their reinterpretation of the Yahwistic text.[18] A closer look at Genesis

5:3, one of the deviant verses in the otherwise orderly and monotonous Priestly genealogy, illustrates this phenomenon. Genesis 5:3 can be seen as a Priestly misreading of Eve's speech in 4:1, as an attempt to refute the possibility of theomorphic begetting by females. Following in God's footsteps, Adam begets a son, Seth, in *his* likeness and image: *va'yoled bidmuto ke'tsalmo*. If in 4:1 Eve's creation is presented by a divine term *(qnh)*, now it is Adam's generative capacities that are defined by an expression which otherwise depicts God's (pro)creation alone. The image of Adam's wife, who is nameless in P, is denied the option of re-presenting itself.

Another more obvious contradiction between the Yahwistic genealogy and the Priestly one leads us back to the question of naming. In the genealogy of P, Adam, rather than Eve, names Seth. Even though Eve is somewhat more humble in her last naming-speech, her role as name-giver apparently is still too powerful for the Priestly writers (who recount only paternal naming)[19]—so much so that they deviate from the recurrent structure of the genealogy to mention the fact that Adam named his son. The primary model for this paternal name-giving seems to be none other than God, whose naming of *ha'adam* is solemnly depicted in 5:2.

My objective is not to turn J into the egalitarian source and P into the sexist version. What I have tried to show throughout my discussion is that patriarchy reigns in both strands. The difference between their respective treatments of femininity is primarily a question of configuration. While Yahwistic texts permit a certain dramatization of the struggle between the sexes, one intertwined with the human-divine conflict, Priestly traditions avoid conflicts just as they avoid narrative. The Priestly discourse is an exact legalistic discourse meant primarily to consecrate rituals and reinforce the power of the divine-human covenant (see Weinfeld 1979). The Priestly God is distant and formal, not quite the sort of deity who engages in conflicts with human beings. If in J humanity violates God's decree in order to acquire divine traits, in P such transgressions are avoided. The creation of man and woman in God's image is presented as part of the divine plan from the outset. Boundaries are boundaries.

Even when the Priestly texts deal with the human level alone, they reveal no interest in the complexities of human relations. Thus, for example, rivalry between siblings, one of J's favorite topics, is smoothed away in the Priestly rendering. As Gunkel puts it, "When it comes to P . . . he makes a clean sweep: he simply omits altogether what is offensive . . . he even goes to the length of maintaining the precise contrary to the tradition: Ishmael and Isaac together peacefully buried their father (xxv. 9), and so did Jacob and Esau (xxxv. 29)" (1964:152). Similarly, rivalry between the sexes is not a major Priestly concern. Man's authority is taken for granted. The Priestly God, when he troubles himself to speak to humanity, speaks solely to the fathers, sending through them messages to the mothers, when necessary. The limited power women end up exerting is not an outcome of a struggle between the sexes, but once again part of a carefully designed plan.

Mixed Languages

Lacking the formal markers we are so accustomed to in modern literature, not to mention its composite character, the Bible surely frustrates any attempt to define authoritative textual boundaries. Considering the problematics of textual delimitation is of course essential to the understanding of modern texts as well, but one should not ignore the specific problems the Bible raises in this respect. It may be difficult to determine where a Faulknerian novel begins or ends, since all of Faulkner's books pertain to the Yoknapatawpha saga, but dealing with a text that is not divided into chapters and parts,[20] a text composed by sundry authors during approximately a dozen centuries, requires a different hermeneutic suspicion.[21] By calling into question the "flaming swords" which Christian theology has treated as the "original" Authorial ending of Creation, I have tried to make a case for a feminist reconstruction of biblical poetics which is historical both in its consideration of biblical ideology and in its attention to the history of the composition of the text. Respect for the otherness of the ancient text, I think, may not only invigorate the critical gesture of feminist biblical criticism but also shed light on the heterogeneity of the Bible, on the complex dialogue between the various manifestations of patriarchal ideology and the antithetical trends which challege the monotheistic repression of femininity. The Tower of Babel, with its monolithic character, is an impossible mode of creation. It is the confounding mixture of dispersed languages which best represents the art of biblical narrative.

~§ 4 §~

Rachel's Dream:
The Female Subplot

Rachel and Jacob have parallel dreams of grandeur. Both strive to surmount the tyranny of time in their respective struggles against their precursors, Leah and Esau. To overcome priority means to overcome nature, to replace a concept from the natural order with one from the spiritual sphere. The biblical master of such revisions is the Creator Himself, whose control over natural phenomena is absolute. What the Bible in fact establishes, from the very first chapter of Genesis, is "a deeper rhythm than that of the annual cycle of the seasons, a rhythm that belongs not to nature but to God" (Josipovici 1988:70). To gain control over natural rhythm is something both Rachel and Jacob seek to do. Their lots, however, are different. In accordance with the official hierarchy of God-man-woman, Jacob's right to imitate God is far greater. What Rachel's prerogative boils down to is to be the mimic of God's mimic in her protest against time—to be Jacob's mirror. She is to be like her husband, but not too like him, just as *ha'adam* is created in God's image, but denied the right to become a deity.

J. P. Fokkelman meticulously maps out the parallels between the stories of Jacob and Rachel. Yet in his quest for symmetry—he goes as far as calling Rachel "Jacoba" (1975:131,135) to accentuate her role as Jacob's "true" female double—he overlooks the difference in the respective status of the male and female plots as well as the concomitant distinction in their modes of development. There is a good deal of dissymmetry in this mirroring, for Jacob's plot is the main plot, while Rachel's narrative is the subplot. This is implied, though never accounted for, in Fokkelman's decision to call Rachel "Jacoba" instead of calling Jacob "Rachel'el," or some other masculinized form of "Rachel."

In exploring the interrelations between the dreams of Rachel and Jacob, I will try to point to the complexity of patriarchal specular dynamics; I will consider both the ways in which dissymmetry is established and the antithetical points in which it is called into question, the rare moments in which the "mirror" refuses to remain empty and specular hierarchies are challenged.[1]

Let us now examine the story of Rachel as it is shaped within the Jacob cycle. At first everything seems to indicate that Rachel, like Jacob, will outdo her elder sibling. To begin with, she has a narratological advantage over Leah. It is Rachel whom Jacob meets first upon arriving at Aram. What is more, he meets her by the well, a favorite setting for biblical betrothal scenes (see Alter 1981:47–62). Taken into the scene through Jacob's eyes, following his sudden ability to roll the huge stone from the mouth of the well and then his weeping as he introduces himself to Rachel, one cannot but assume that such confused behavior is indicative of love at first sight. Leah is introduced only later, in a belated expository remark inserted in the midst of initial negotiations between Jacob and Laban.

> Because thou art my brother, shouldest thou therefore serve me for nought? tell me, what shall thy wages be? And Laban had two daughters: the name of the elder was Leah, and the name of the younger was Rachel. Leah was tender eyed; but Rachel was beautiful and well favoured. And Jacob loved

Rachel; and said, I will serve thee seven years for Rachel thy younger daughter. And Laban said, It is better that I give her to thee, than that I should give her to another man: abide with me. And Jacob served seven years for Rachel; and they seemed unto him but a few days, for the love he had to her.   (Gen. 29:15–20)

Although this interpolated remark changes the picture, for now we are dealing with two potential brides, Rachel's success still seems ensured. She is far more beautiful than her elder "weak-eyed" (as the Hebrew may be construed) sister; and Jacob, now that his feelings are explicitly revealed, is wholly enamored of her, turning seven years into a few days through the force of his love. Then unexpectedly we discover that the reversal of the primogeniture law, a pivotal phenomenon in in the Bible and particularly in Genesis, doesn't quite work when women are involved. On the wedding night Jacob had dreamed of for seven years Leah is passed off to him as Rachel. The natural order is maintained: the elder sister comes first, the younger must wait.

And Jacob said unto Laban, Give me my wife, for my days are fulfilled, that I may go in unto her. And Laban gathered together all the men of the place, and made a feast. And it came to pass in the evening, that he took Leah his daughter, and brought her to him; and he went in unto her . . . And it came to pass, that in the morning, behold, it was Leah: and he said to Laban, What is this thou hast done unto me? did not I serve with thee for Rachel? wherefore then hast thou beguiled me? And Laban said, It must not be so done in our country, to give the younger before the firstborn.   (Gen. 29:21–26)

Laban's move, as many have noted, serves as a symmetrical punishment for Jacob's cunning usurpation of his elder brother's birthright. Just as the blind Isaac "misfeels" Jacob, so the young trickster, blinded by love, becomes a victim of an inverted "bed trick" as he lies with the elder sister instead of the younger one.[2] The female subplot, at this point, is wholly at the service of Jacob's education. Accordingly, the perspectives of Leah and Rachel on this exchange are withheld.

The Young Barren One versus the Elder Cowife

Despite Laban's trickery, Rachel remains in the position of the chosen one. Jacob's love for her surpasses his attachment to her sister. He works seven more years for the sake of his beloved. Marriage, however, offers no sweet end to Rachel's hardships. A new problem arises when God provides Leah (the "hated" wife) with sons, while Rachel's womb remains closed. The motif of sibling rivalry thus blends with a recurrent element in the annunciation type-scene: the struggle between the loved barren one and the less loved fertile cowife.[3] The merging of the two motifs is smooth, for the underlying pattern remains the same. The belatedness which characterizes Rachel's birth and marriage is now apparent in her deferred motherhood. Similarly, Leah's priority in emerging from the womb is recapitulated in her capacity to bear long before Rachel is able to give birth.

The split between the two sisters is fleshed out when the narrator at last gives us access to their feelings. As if to underline Leah's fertility, the first mode of discourse allotted to her is a predominantly maternal discourse in biblical narrative, that is, naming-speeches.

And Leah conceived, and bare a son, and she called his name Reuben: for she said, Surely the Lord hath looked upon my affliction; now therefore my husband will love me. And she conceived again, and bare a son; and said, Because the Lord hath heard that I was hated, he hath therefore given me this

son also: and she called his name Simeon. And she conceived
again, and bare a son; and said, Now this time will my husband be joined unto me, because I have born him three sons:
therefore was his name called Levi.   (Gen. 29: 32–34)

While joyfully naming her firstborn, Leah expresses the
hope that her success as a mother will enable her to win her
husband's love. Yet the reiteration of this wish in the following naming-speeches intimates that not much has changed in
Jacob's attitude toward her. Her pain at being neglected seems
to increase from one birth to the next.

To the extent that these speeches are implicitly meant as
taunts directed at the barren Rachel, they hit the mark. In the
verse which follows the description of Leah's tireless bearing
and naming of son after son, we receive an explicit statement
of the narrator regarding Rachel's feelings: "And when
Rachel saw that she bare Jacob no children, Rachel envied her
sister" (Gen. 30:1).

When Rachel's voice finally bursts out, it is very bold,
impulsive, and painful: "Give me children, or else I die"
(ibid.), she demands of Jacob. Her desperate craving for offspring is inflamed by envy. In but a few words she conveys
the unbearable agony of being a barren woman: childlessness
means death. Rachel can wait no longer. Working against
time, she is willing to do anything she can to overcome the
retardation which marks her life. She ends up giving Jacob
her maid Bilhah, hoping to "be built" (*ve'ibane gam anokhi
mimena*, Gen. 30:3) in this vicarious manner. And as Bilhah
gives birth "upon her mistress' knees," Rachel gains access to
the discourse which previously was solely within Leah's
reach: naming-speeches.

That the rivalry between the sisters is meant to mirror
the struggle of Jacob and Esau in the main plot becomes conspicuous in Rachel's speech upon Naphtali's birth: "With
great wrestlings [*naftuley Elohim*, lit. a contest of God] have I

wrestled [*niftalti*] with my sister, and I have prevailed: and she called his name Naphtali" (Gen. 30:8). Her speech anticipates Jacob's struggle with the angel, which is inextricably connected with his struggle with Esau (see Fokkelman 1975:135–136). Just as Jacob "prevails" (note the recurrence of the word) in his wrestling "with God and men" (Gen. 32:28), so Rachel, in an extremely condensed version of her counterpart's struggle, claims to have overcome her sister "with great wrestlings," with wrestlings of God. Once again Rachel is supposedly in Jacob's position, but not quite so. To begin with, God's role in this contest is solely figurative. Rachel's evocation of God's name to define the magnitude of the struggle with her sister may disclose a desire for a different plot, a plot in which, as in Jacob's case, one is deemed worthy of struggling with the Ultimate Precursor in the process of making "the elder serve the younger" (Gen. 25:23). But God's intervention in Rachel's story remains marginal. The limited role God chooses to play in women's lives may in fact be construed as the theological correlate for the fragility of their dreams.

Even more striking—and this point has been continuously overlooked by biblical exegetes—is the fact that Rachel's triumph over her sister is no more than a boast of questionable validity. After all, the son she names is Bilhah's son. Her womb is still closed. This naming-speech is more the delusion of a desperate woman, trying to find comfort in the offspring of her maid.

Much like the *ficelle*—Henry James's term for a secondary character who serves to set off the protagonist's representation—Rachel runs breathless "beside the coach" of the "true agent," but neither manages to get her "foot on the step," nor to cease "for a moment to tread the dusty road" (1986:53).[4] In Rachel's case her foot seems very close to the step, but, for one reason or another, she misses it and again ends up running behind time.[5] This is why Rachel's struggle serves as a fine foil to the splendor of life in the "coach," where Jacob actually prevails in his struggle against belatedness.

Exchanging Plots

Mutual despair eventually leads the sisters to a dialogue. "And Reuben went in the days of wheat harvest, and found mandrakes in the field, and brought them unto his mother Leah. Then Rachel said to Leah, Give me, I pray thee, of thy son's mandrakes. And she said unto her, Is it a small matter that thou hast taken my husband? and wouldest thou take away my son's mandrakes also? And Rachel said, Therefore he shall lie with thee to night for thy son's mandrakes." (Gen. 30:14–15).

The dialogue between the two women is tense, but it is a dialogue. Given the predominant use of dialogue in biblical narrative, it is striking to notice how rarely one finds two women conversing. (No exchange whatsoever takes place in the representation of the analogous relations of Sarah-Hagar and Hannah-Peninah.) The angry exchange between Leah and Rachel eventually leads them to strike a deal. Each gives up her particular prerogative in order to gain the prize she lacks. Rachel trades Jacob for a night, while Leah gives her sister the mandrakes, the fruit which promises fertility, the object which metonymically represents the son: *duda'ey beni* (the mandrakes of my son). This deal evokes the notorious deal between Jacob and Esau (Gen. 25:29–34). In both cases, as Fokkelman points out (1975:140), the younger person initiates the deal; in both narratives the struggle is for leadership. But whereas Esau, with his terrible craving for lentils, is no match for Jacob, Leah is a rival whose merit cannot be ignored. She benefits from the deal at least as much as Rachel does. Under God's auspices both sisters become pregnant, although Leah is first, perhaps as an implied criticism of Rachel's willingness to use dubious means to acquire fertility.[6]

Interestingly, the story of the mandrakes is the one conspicuous spot in this double plot where a reversal of hierarchies is at work. Jacob here descends to the humiliating position of being a token of exchange between two women. To
use James's metaphor once again, Jacob is, for a moment,
thrown off the coach to experience what running breathless
on a dusty road feels like. Patriarchal specular logic is ridi-
culed. The eponymous father of Israel becomes the faithful
mirror of his wives: the two sisters were exactly in this position when they were circulated between Laban and Jacob in
Genesis 29. Jacob is not even allowed to respond to Leah's
stinging remark: "Thou must come in unto me; for surely I
have hired thee with my son's mandrakes." He follows her
obediently. "And he lay with her that night" (Gen. 30:16).

Paradoxically, being momentarily in the position of the
other turns out to be to Jacob's advantage insofar as it enhances the "building" of his house. The following Yahwistic
episode may be seen as an attempt to boost Jacob's ego.
From serving as means of circulation between the two sisters,
from being in a female position, he now manipulates the mating of Laban's flocks. Using rods as stimuli, he manages to
increase the numbers of the speckled sheep and goats (the rare
type) which Laban allotted to him: "And Jacob took him rods
of green poplar . . . and pilled white strakes in them . . . And
he set the rods which he had pilled before the flocks in the
gutters in the watering troughs when the flocks came to
drink, that they should conceive when they came to drink.
And the flocks conceived before the rods, and brought forth
cattle ringstraked, speckled, and spotted" (Gen. 30:37–39).

Fertility, which in the previous scene was controlled by
women, is now wholly in Jacob's hands. His success as a
shepherd seems to have bearing on his virility, especially in
light of the fact that the names Rachel and Leah mean "ewe"
and "cow." (Jacob makes a pun regarding this issue in Gen.
31:38: "This twenty years have I been with thee; thy ewes

[*rechelekha*] and thy she goats have not cast their young.")
Jacob is back in business, thriving more than ever. "And the
man increased exceedingly" *(vayifrots ha'ish me'od me'od)* and
had, in this order, "much cattle, and maidservants, and men-
servants, and camels, and asses" (Gen. 30:43). At last he can
return home to Canaan; he is ready for the decisive encounter
with Esau.

Joining Forces

In order to leave Laban's household Jacob must have the con-
sent of Rachel and Leah. The three meet in the field. Jacob
opens with a detailed depiction of Laban's continual abuse of
him and ends with God's request that he return to Canaan
(see Gen. 31:5–13). The sisters respond with one voice: "And
Rachel and Leah answered and said unto him, Is there yet any
portion or inheritance for us in our father's house? Are we
not counted of him strangers? for he hath sold us, and hath
quite devoured also our money. For all the riches which God
hath taken from our father, that is ours, and our children's:
now then, whatsoever God hath said unto thee, do" (Gen.
31:14–16).

The two have learned to cooperate in times of distress.
Enraged by Laban's usurpation of their inheritance and by
their status as *nokhriyot* (foreigners) in his household, they do
not hesitate to join forces with Jacob against their father. In
this case all three have parallel histories. They are all victims
of Laban's wheeling and dealing, and, even more interesting,
all three are foreigners: Jacob is literally so, while the sisters
are estranged on a figurative level. Up until now the text
focused on Laban's merciless exploitation of Jacob and the
latter's attempt to deceive the deceiver. Now we get a
glimpse of what has been withheld: the attitude of the sisters
with respect to their father's deeds. At this point their provocative perspective may be revealed, for it offers a critique

of the oppression of women within, to use Bal's terms, the "patrilocal" system (domination of father or father-in-law), just as the transition to a "virilocal" system (domination of husband) needs to be legitimized.[7] The journey from Aram to Canaan is the concomitant geographical move.

Esther Fuchs suggests that the sisters' response is meant to shed a more positive light on Jacob's motives. Whereas Jacob emphasizes God as the ultimate reason for his desire to leave Laban's household, "his wives stress the financial aspect as their primary concern" (1988:72). A contrast is thus set up between Jacob's piety and the sisters' pragmatism. Fuchs's insistence on dissymmetry in her analysis of the encounter in the field is valuable, but her observations are oversimplified. Here as elsewhere she tends, as Bal puts it, to remain "within the moralistic isotopy of good and evil" (1988c:143). Fuchs repeats, in other words, a common patriarchal gesture by regarding the dichotomy of good and bad as parallel to male and female, overlooking the ways in which biblical texts challenge such rigid divisions.

To say that Leah and Rachel are morally inferior because of their financial concerns is to ignore both the value system at stake and the fact of their being totally at the mercy of such socioeconomic strictures. What is problematic here is not the preoccupation with economic issues—wealth is an unmistakable ingredient of election in the Bible—but rather the means by which property is attained. In this respect Fuchs seems to have fallen under the spell of Jacob's rhetoric. "And it came to pass," says Jacob,

> at the time that the cattle conceived, that I lifted up mine eyes, and saw in a dream, and, behold, the rams which leaped upon the cattle were ringstraked, speckled, and grisled. And the angel of God spake unto me in a dream, saying, Jacob: and I said, Here am I. And he said, Lift up now thine eyes, and see, all the rams which leap upon the cattle are ringstraked, speckled, and grisled: for I have seen all that Laban doeth unto

thee . . . now arise, get thee out from this land, and return
unto the land of thy kindred. (Gen. 31:10–13).

But Jacob does not have to be taken as a reliable narrator.
As we have seen in Genesis 30:37–43, the mating of the flocks
was orchestrated not by an angel but by Jacob's rods. There
is an ironic gap between Jacob's deeds and words. He is, one
should bear in mind, trying to impress his wives.

Does he succeed? One cannot be sure. There is something about the sisters' response which mocks Jacob's sense
of self-importance and self-righteousness, much as a "clown
subplot" (see Levin 1971) often parodies the seriousness with
which the king regards himself. Rachel and Leah translate
Jacob's long calculated legalistic speech into a brief, blunt,
and spicy depiction of Laban's greed. Laban, they claim, is
more than a dishonest deceiver; he is a covetous monster who
would stop neither at selling his own daughters nor at
"devouring" their money *(vayokhal gam a'khol 'et kaspenu)*.

The sisters speak with one voice against their greedy
father, yet it seems to be primarily Rachel's voice. This is at
least one way to account for the order of presentation: Rachel
before Leah (Gen. 31:14). The following story, in which
Rachel steals the *terafim* (household gods), augments the
notion that she is the instigator of the sisters' rebellion against
Laban. Here too is a scene that curiously evokes a central episode in Jacob's life. In light of the fact that possession of the
household gods could serve as the symbolic token of leadership in a given estate (as is evident in the Nuzi documents;
see Speiser 1964), what Rachel is after in this case is analogous
to what Jacob cunningly wrests from his blind old father. The
verbal marker linking the two episodes is the verb *mishesh*
(feel, or touch) (see Fokkelman 1975:170 and Fishbane 1979:
56). When Laban enters Rachel's tent, he "feels" all her
belongings, but fails to find the *terafim*. Stricken by male fear
of menstruation (see Bal 1988c:151), he accepts Rachel's

request to remain seated: "And she said to her father, Let it not displease my lord that I cannot rise up before thee; for the custom of women is upon me" (Gen. 31:35). "Feeling" turns out once again to be an unreliable protection against the trickery of one's offspring.

Rachel's act is directed not only against her father; it may also be seen as yet another manifestation of the rivalry between the two sisters. Just as Jacob's tricking of Isaac is meant to secure his priority vis-à-vis Esau, so Rachel's tricking of Laban is bound up with her ongoing desire to prevail over her elder sister. Although Rachel is both a mother and the beloved wife at this point, her son isn't Jacob's firstborn, which is why the *terafim* are needed. Belatedness is still a problem. The struggle between the sisters isn't quite over, for the law that institutionalizes natural order threatens Joseph's status. "If a man have two wives, one beloved, and another hated, and they have born him children, both the beloved and the hated; and if the firstborn son be hers that was hated: Then it shall be, when he maketh his sons to inherit that which he hath, that he may not make the son of the beloved firstborn before the son of the hated, which is indeed the firstborn" (Deut. 21:15–16).

This law, however, is often violated in the annunciation type-scene. Thus Sarah's son, rather than Hagar's son, assumes the position of the firstborn, just as Hannah's son, rather than Peninah's firstborn, becomes God's messenger. As the loved barren one, Rachel seems to have the potential of being the elected mother of the chosen son; but this privilege is taken away from her just when she is about to reach her destination.

Rachel's Death

Rachel's death, perhaps even more than her life, encapsulates her unfulfilled yearnings, her tragic exile. She dies on the way—not far from Ephrath, but not fully there. Bearing in mind that Ephrath is Bethlehem (Gen. 35:19), the location of her tomb is not without significance. This liminal locus intimates that she makes it to the threshold of the royal city but is not allowed to enter. The future Davidic dynasty does not spring from her sons, but from Judah, Leah's fourth son (see Alter 1983:123).

Rachel's final naming-speech marks her agony. "Son of my sorrow" (*ben-'oni,* Gen. 35:18) she calls her second son upon dying. She who desperately cried "Give me children, or else I die" ironically dies upon bearing a son. Jacob quickly changes the name to "Benjamin," son of my right hand, perhaps to protect the newly born child from such a gloomy name, perhaps in an attempt to mitigate the pain which characterizes his beloved's life, or possibly as a promise to the dying Rachel that at least in the case of her sons (regardless of the lot of Leah's sons), the younger shall prevail, just as one's right hand prevails. Later, when blessing Joseph's sons, he will similarly switch hands, placing the right hand on the younger Ephraim and his left on Menashe.

But why does Rachel die in the prime of her life? Rabbinic interpretations stress the fatal impact of Jacob's curse.[8] "With whomsoever thou findest thy gods, let him not live" (Gen. 31:32), says Jacob in response to Laban's accusation that he stole the household gods. Although the text goes on to mitigate Jacob's harshness by making clear that "Jacob knew not that Rachel had stolen them," one may well wonder whether Jacob, not unlike Jephthah, should have been aware of the possible consequences of his speech act.[9] Jacob knows only too well that Rachel has supported his "stealing away" (Gen. 31:20) from Laban's household. It would not take too great a leap of the imagination to surmise that Rachel might have ventured to do some literal stealing. I am not trying to cast doubt on Jacob's great love for the woman he adored at first sight, but there is something about Rachel's ambitions which makes her threatening even for Jacob.

Rachel, as we have seen, ridicules Jacob when swapping him for Reuben's mandrakes. But this tendency can be traced, if to a lesser extent, back to their very first dialogue, where she implicitly blames Jacob for her barrenness. Her cry "Give me children, or else I die" (Gen. 30:1) at first may seem an irrational accusation of Jacob for something he couldn't possibly be responsible for. And indeed, Jacob's angry response reinforces this notion: "Am I in God's stead, who hath withheld from thee the fruit of the womb?" (Gen. 30:2). Rachel, however, is not mistaken in her choice of addressee, as the insightful midrashic elaboration of this exchange makes clear. "*Am I in God's stead, who hath withheld from thee the fruit of the womb?* 'From thee he withheld it, but not from me.' Said she to him: 'Did then your father act so to your mother? Did he not gird up his loins by her?' 'He had no children,' he retorted, 'whereas I have children.' 'And did not your grandfather [Abraham] have children,' she pursued, 'yet he too girded up his loins by Sarah?'" (Genesis Rabba, LXXI. 7).

Given the examples of his paternal precursors, who prayed for the sake of their barren wives and succeeded in procuring divine intervention, Jacob should have tried to use his higher position in relation to God to help bring about the opening of his wife's womb. Rachel's exposure of his ineptness, in other words, is justifiable, which is what makes Jacob so angry.

Once Jacob is on the way to Canaan and the struggle with Laban is basically over, Rachel's audacity is not as beneficial as before. His curse may thus be perceived as the expression of an unwitting wish to set limits to his counterpart's plot. She is a fine mirror, but at times her mirroring comes close to self-representation. At times she goes too far in striving to become a subject, like her counterpart, which is why her voice must be repressed.[10]

To be sure, Jacob will mourn Rachel desperately for the rest of his life (see Gen. 48:7), and will love her sons, Benjamin and especially Joseph, more than Leah's sons.[11] Yet when Jacob himself approaches death, he will ask to lie at Leah's side (Gen. 49:31); he will end up preferring the traditional burial place, where Abraham buried Sarah and Isaac buried Rebekah, to being buried as an outsider, on the road, with Rachel (see Steinsaltz 1984). This is Leah's ultimate triumph.

Difference in Development

Rachel remains the black sheep of the family. Unlike Jacob, she is never given a chance to be transformed. Nor does her relationship with Leah ever reach the point of an explicit reconciliation, as is the case with Jacob and Esau. The two issues are not unrelated. Jacob's inner transformation is inextricably bound up with his capacity to cope with his brother. Their reconciliation can take place only after he struggles with the angel, after he sheds the name Jacob (a derivation of the verb *'akv,* meaning "to twist" or "trick") and acquires from his divine opponent a new name, Israel. This new name marks a change in his character, a rebirth, for he seems to enter a higher state of being upon his designation as the eponymic father of the nation.[12] I am not suggesting that Jacob becomes angelic after his nocturnal struggle, nor that the reconciliation between the brothers is innocent of tension. Nevertheless, change, albeit limited, is possible in the male realm.

Transformation is the hallmark of the biblical hero, as Erich Auerbach notes in his seminal "Odysseus' Scar":

> But what a road, what a fate, lie between the Jacob who cheated his father out of his blessing and the old man whose

favorite son has been torn to pieces by a wild beast!—between David the harp player, persecuted by his lord's jealousy, and the old king, surrounded by violent intrigues, whom Abishag the Shunnamite warmed in his bed, and he knew her not! The old man, of whom we know how he has become what he is, is more of an individual than the young man; for it is only during the course of an eventful life that men are differentiated into full individuality; and it is this history of a personality which the Old Testament presents to us as the formation undergone by those whom God has chosen to be examples. Fraught with their development, sometimes even aged to the verge of dissolution, they show a distinct stamp of individuality entirely foreign to the Homeric heroes.   (1974:17–18)

Female characters, however, are not so "fraught with development." Their textual life span is limited. With the exception of Eve, we have no scene which depicts the birth of the heroine, let alone rebirth. The biblical woman appears on stage only when she is marriageable, and her stay there is determined, generally speaking, by the impact of her maternal position on the status of her (favorite) son. Rachel actually dies in childbirth, but other biblical mothers simply vanish from the scene once their offspring are on their own. Their function as a foil to the men in their lives precludes the possibility of significant change; it limits the capacity of their dreams to shape reality.

Dreams and Reality

In "The Relation of the Poet to Day-Dreaming," Freud analyzes the fulfillment of wishes in popular novels and romances. Such texts, he claims, have a "marked characteristic": "They all have a hero who is the center of interest, for whom the author tries to win our sympathy by every possible means, and whom he places under the protection of a special providence" (1958:50).

The hero of course is bound to undergo numerous hardships, but we may maintain a feeling of security that he will
find a way out of every dangerous situation, for we share the
hero's own conviction of invincibility—best rendered in the
expression "Nothing can happen to me!" Freud goes on to
suggest that "this significant mark of invulnerability very
clearly betrays—His Majesty the Ego, the hero of all day-
dreams and all novels" (p. 51).

The Hebrew Bible, as Gabriel Josipovici aptly shows,
does not offer the comforts of fulfillment found in fairy tales
and romances. It "takes pleasure in allowing . . . dreams their
full force, but then sets them against reality—the dreams of
others and the facts of life, such as failure and death"
(1988:193). Josipovici's observations hold true for both
Rachel and Jacob. What they do not account for, however, is
the different ratios between ambition and reality in the
respective lives of the primary vehicles of divine election, and
of the secondary ones.

Jacob, like the hero Freud describes, is placed in a central
position "under the protection of a special providence." He is
God's unmistakable elect, and as such he manages to realize
what he tried to do already upon grabbing Esau's heel: to
reverse natural order. But Jacob is not invulnerable. He is not
in the position of God, which is in a sense the position fairy
tales allow "His Majesty the Ego" to attain. Jacob's decisive
victory over Esau does not enable him to live "happily ever
after." The great trickster is tricked time and again: first by
Laban and then by his own sons.[13] What is more, he must
yield to death. And the length of life given him is a final frustration. "The years of my sojourn [on earth] are one hundred
and thirty. Few and hard have been the years of my life, nor
do they come up to the life-spans of my fathers during their
sojourns" (Gen. 47:9 in the new JPS translation). The realization of one dream is no guarantee that other dreams will be

realized. In comparison with his two paternal precursors, Jacob feels something of a loser. They had better control over time; their life spans were greater.

But seen against the background of Rachel's premature death, Jacob's lot does not appear too bleak. The restrictions reality sets up for Rachel's dreams are far greater. Although God occasionally "remembers" Rachel (Gen. 30:22), her story seems to be the obverse negative of "nothing can happen to me." The phrase that best characterizes Rachel's posture might well be, in Nancy Miller's terms, "a variant of Murphy's law: If anything can go wrong, it will" (1981:40). Ambition is primarily a patriarchal prerogative. A female character who tries to fulfill her ambitious dreams, to protest against time's tyranny, runs her head against a wall.

Rachel's dream, however, is not doomed to total frustration. In a remarkable manner she has always managed to gain much admiration for her daring aspirations and compassion for her tragic failures. She may be the black sheep of the family, but despite, or because of, this role, she has never ceased to be the favorite matriarch in Jewish tradition. This is already evident in Jeremiah, who selects Rachel, and not Leah, as the mother of the nation, as the one who is best suited to accompany Jacob in his position as the eponymous father.

A voice was heard in Ramah, lamentation and bitter weeping; Rahel weeping for her children refused to be comforted for her children, because they were not. Thus saith the Lord; Refrain thy voice from weeping, and thine eyes from tears: for thy work shall be rewarded, saith the Lord; and they shall come again from the land of the enemy. And there is hope in thine end, saith the Lord, that thy children shall come again to their own border.   (Jer. 31:15–17)

In Jeremiah's famous prophecy Rachel is allowed to transcend time. Her voice rises from the dead to cry on behalf of the exiled.

❧ 5 ❧

Zipporah and the Struggle
for Deliverance

One of the most antithetical Yahwistic texts in biblical narrative is the story of "The Bridegroom of Blood" (Exod. 4:24–26). Upon making his way back to Egypt, something strange happens to Moses, which runs contrary to the preceding divine message. God, who has just sent Moses back to Egypt to do wonders before Pharaoh and the people, seeks to kill His messenger at a night lodging on the way. The enigma thickens when Zipporah takes a flint, circumcises her son and touches "his feet" with the foreskin, saying: "A bridegroom of blood art thou to me."[1] What follows is by far the most perplexing moment in this strange night: Yahweh succumbs to Zipporah's magical act and withdraws. Moses is saved.

This cryptic story (it is only three verses long!) raises numerous questions. Why does Yahweh wish to kill Moses? What keeps Moses from reacting? Why is circumcision necessary? Why does Zipporah perform the circumcision? Whose feet are touched with the foreskin? What is the meaning of Zipporah's incantation? Who is the "bridegroom of blood"? Why does Yahweh withdraw?

The predominant tendency of biblical exegetes has been to decipher this enigmatic text by analyzing it in relation to its textual surroundings. Many scholars have suggested that

the preceding verses—in which Yahweh tells Moses of the
death that will befall Pharaoh's firstborn if Pharaoh does not
let go of God's firstborn, namely, Israel (Exod. 21–23)—may
serve as a clue to the enigma. Thus, Moshe Greenberg perceptively argues that God's nocturnal attack as well as His
preceding message, "turn out to be premonitions of things to
come depicted in intensely personal terms" (1969:117). First,
God foretells and explicates the final plague against firstborns
by means of a father-son metaphor. Second, His assault on
Moses foreshadows the danger the nation as a whole will be
exposed to during the last plague. And just as Yahweh is
warded off through a blood rite in Exodus 4, so Israel will be
saved from the deadly touch of the "destroyer" *(hamashchit)*
by the paschal blood rite in Exodus 12.

Another common interpretation sees "The Bridegroom
of Blood" as yet another variation on the theme of Moses'
refusal to accept his call (see Buber 1988, Blau 1956; Talmon
1954). And indeed the preceding episode, Exodus 3:1–4:17,
which is usually attributed to JE, offers an account of God's
revelation at the bush and Moses' stubborn attempts to escape
the role of national liberator. "Who am I," asks Moses, "that
I should go unto Pharaoh, and that I should bring forth the
children of Israel out of Egypt?" (Exod. 3:11). In response to
his anxious question, God promises to be with him. Moses,
however, refuses to yield. He demands to know the name of
his Sender. God dramatically reveals His Name—*'ehye 'asher
'ehye,* "I am that I am"—but even this does not suffice, for
Moses raises another problem: the incredulity of the people.
Tireless, he goes on to suggest that he lacks the necessary
eloquence: "but I am slow of speech, and of a slow tongue"
(Exod. 4:10). Finally Moses simply requests that God look
for someone else. But this last attempt to withdraw only kin-
dles divine anger. God loses His patience and dispatches
Moses despite his reservations.

Similarly, in a Priestly version in Exodus 6, the reluctant hero manages—very briefly this time—to express his opposition to the call. "How then," he asks, "shall Pharaoh hear me, who am of uncircumcised lips?" (Exod. 6:12; see also Exod. 6:30).

Moses' arguments with God in these accounts become an eerily physical combat in "The Bridegroom of Blood," for here God's anger is conveyed by means of concrete violence, and His insistence on having complete possession of the one He has chosen turns into a murder attempt. Furthermore, in accordance with the concretization of the struggle, (un)circumcision is more than a figure of speech. In the Yahwistic version a foreskin is literally cut, blood flows, and a strange ritual takes place.

While these intertextual ties indeed shed light on the possible meaning of "The Bridegroom of Blood," they do not account for Zipporah's enigmatic role, nor do they explain the striking otherness of the story.

Female Saviors

Why then does Zipporah loom so large in this nocturnal combat? To understand better the power she holds in her hands, some underexamined intertextual connections in Exodus need to be examined. In saving Moses from the wrath of Yahweh, Zipporah, I contend, follows in the footsteps of a whole array of female characters in Exodus 1–2 who venture to trick Pharaoh as they rescue Moses from the deadly royal decree.[2]

I begin with Shiphrah and Puah, the two midwives (even though their action is not explicitly related to the saving of Moses) who violate Pharaoh's decree, justifying themselves with midwives' tales: "And the king of Egypt called for the midwives, and said unto them, Why have ye done this thing,

and have saved the men children alive? And the midwives
said unto Pharaoh, Because the Hebrew women are not as
the Egyptian women; for they are lively, and are delivered ere
the midwives come in unto them" (1:18–19).

The midwives tell Pharaoh what he wants to hear, and
by handling him in this manner they save the newly born
Hebrews as well as their own skins. They deceive Pharaoh
by confirming his racist anxieties concerning the proliferation
of the Hebrew slaves. Relying on a common racist notion,
according to which the Other is closer to Nature, Shiphrah
and Puah claim that the Hebrew women need no midwives
for, unlike Egyptian women, they are animal-like (*chayot,*
translated by King James as "lively") and can give birth without professional help.

Similarly, Moses' mother fools Pharaoh by feigning to
fulfill his decree. Upon exposing her son, Yocheved ironically follows the letter of the law! (see Ackerman 1974:90).
As Abarbanel already suggested: "The good woman figured
shrewdly that perhaps her son was fated to be thrown into
the Nile. She therefore contrived to have him thrown into
it as to satisfy his destiny" (quoted in Greenberg 1969:39).
Miriam, who guards the ark from a distance, is of course an
accomplice in this scheme.

Finally, Pharaoh is tricked by his own daughter. The
princess rescues and raises an "illegal alien" right under her
father's nose. Her naming-speech highlights her rebellious
move. "And she called his name Moses [*Moshe*]: and she said,
Because I drew him out [*meshitihu*] of the water" (Exod.
2:10). By calling her adopted son *Moshe* and linking his name
to the Hebrew verb *masha* (to draw out), she passes on to him
the power to draw out against Pharaoh's will. Just as she drew
out of the water a weak foundling despite her father's law, so
Moses will eventually draw his people out of Pharaonic
bondage. (Isaiah underscores the princess' message by designating Moses as *moshe 'amo,* "the drawer-out of the nation,"

63:11).[3] Her naming-speech thus calls for the liberation of the oppressed; it foretells and instigates the birth of a nation. Perhaps the Egyptian meaning of the name serves as a cover for this revolutionary proposition. Etymologically speaking, *moshe* is an Egyptian word meaning "child of." It often appears as the final element in theophoric names such as Ahmosis or Thutmosis. Through this bilingual pun, the princess may, in the same breath, be paying lip service to the dominant discourse and undermining Pharaonic authority.

Like her precursors, Zipporah placates the attacker by complying partially and cunningly with his whims. Her strategy is synecdochic: *pars pro toto,* a foreskin and a touch of blood for the victim's life (see Talmon 1954:93). Through this ritual of circumcision and the spreading ("touching") of the blood, Zipporah transforms harmful violence into a regulated expression of violence, turning blood from a potential signifier of death into a beneficial substance that wards off danger (see Girard 1977).

In psychoanalytic terms Zipporah provides Yahweh with a fine "symbolic substitution." Freud, as one recalls, defines circumcision as a "symbolic substitute of castration, a punishment which the primeval father dealt his sons long ago out of the fullness of his power; and whosoever accepted this symbol showed by so doing that he was ready to submit to the father's will, although it was at the cost of a painful sacrifice" (1967:156).

What Freud neglects to take into account both in his depiction of the primal horde and in his treatment of the "family romance"[4] is that women (and mothers in particular)—despite, or rather because of, their powerlessness—may have an important role in teaching the weak and threatened young sons how to trick hostile oppressors, how to submit to paternal will and at the same time usurp the father's position.[5]

Back to the Ark

But why is Moses so passive and dumbfounded during this night on the road to Egypt? He could have joined forces with Zipporah, just as Jacob plays a significant role in his mother's scheme against Isaac. Better still, he could have wrestled with the divine being, just as Jacob struggled with the angel on his way back to Canaan (a parallel rite of passage).[6] Moses, however, falls behind the model of the eponymous patriarch; he seems paralyzed by the anxieties and doubts that haunt him at this liminal phase in his career. Too frightened to assume the role of the father of the nation, the role God assigns to him, Moses finds himself, as it were, back in the ark, in the regressive position of a helpless infant whose well-being is determined by others. The blurred demarcation between Moses and his son underlines this regressive move. The referent of "him" in verse 24 is undefined. Given the fact that Moses is the addressee in the previous passage, I have (like most commentators) regarded Moses—and not his son—to be the victim of divine wrath, but strictly speaking, the identity of the victim is undetermined. It becomes far more difficult to tell the father and son apart in verse 25, where either one could be the referent of "his feet."[7]

The resurgence of the pattern whereby Moses is threatened by a father figure and saved by a woman in "The Bridegroom of Blood" marks a sudden collapse of the heroic paradigm. Moses was surely on a safer road to conventional heroism when he rescued Zipporah and her sisters from the shepherds in Exodus 2. On this fatal night, however, heroism, "the expression and justification of patriarchy" (Bal 1987:37), turns out to be a most fragile concept. Moses seems incapable of making the final leap from the position of the son to that of the father, and accordingly, Zipporah plays a traditional maternal role with regard to not only her son but also Moses.

Zipporah's swift and powerful move to the center of the stage thus challenges the patriarchal presuppositions of heroism. While Moses is aghast, she moves quickly, takes a flint, cuts her son's foreskin, designates Moses as her "bridegroom of blood," and courageously confronts Yahweh.

And yet Moses' return to the ark turns out to be more conducive to his heroism than it may at first seem. It ends up leading to a rebirth of sorts, a transformation. For what Zipporah reminds Moses is something he had already learned from his former female saviors: that against all odds the weak may defeat the strong. As a powerless budding hero and the would-be father of an oppressed and belated nation, what Moses needs indeed to acquire at this point is the capacity to struggle against all odds as well as the capacity to use the weapon of the weak: cunning.[8] Zipporah apparently succeeds in releasing him from some of his anxieties, for right after this strange event he finally dares to approach Pharaoh and request that the king allow the children of Israel to hold a feast unto their God in the wilderness (see Exod. 5). This is Moses' first trick! He neglects to mention the fact that they have no intention of returning to Egypt after the feast is over (see Loewenstamm 1965:48).

The Bridegroom of Blood

Zipporah's reiterated statement remains one of the most perplexing parts of the story. Commentators are divided as to the identity of the *hatan damim* (bridegroom of blood). Some have suggested that Zipporah addresses her son. The word *hatan,* they argue, needs to be understood not in the sense of "bridegroom," but rather in light of its Arabic cognate *hatana* (to circumcise). Zipporah, according to this approach, ceremoniously marks her son as a "circumcised one," as one who is protected by the blood of circumcision.

But the common biblical use of the word *hatan* as "bridegroom" should not be ignored.[9] I find Umberto Cassuto's interpretation the most convincing. "At that moment," claims Cassuto, "Zipporah turned to Moses *and said* to him, *Surely a blood-bridegroom are you to me,* meaning, I am delivering you from death—indeed, I am restoring you to life— by means of our son's blood; and your return to life makes you, as it were, my bridegroom a second time, this time a blood-bridegroom, a bridegroom acquired through blood" (1967:60–61). Zipporah is celebrating her triumph over death, her successful restoration of her beloved to life, her power to make blood mean life and protection. "In thy blood, Live," says God to the newly born and deserted nation in Ezekiel 16:6, and this is precisely what Zipporah seems to be saying, at this moment of reunion with Moses, to the man whose history is inextricably connected with that of the nation. Unlike Ezekiel's adjuration, however, Zipporah's words sound like an incantation, as if part of a magical ceremony.

Shemaryahu Talmon (1954) attempts to smooth over Zipporah's strange role in this ceremony by suggesting that the word *ly* (usually translated as "to me") is an abbreviation of *le-YHWH* (to YHWH). What Zipporah is saying, according to Talmon, is "a bridegroom of blood art thou to YHWH," which is why the story needs to be perceived as representing a primary covenantal bonding between Moses and Yahweh. The covenantal aspect, he goes on to suggest, is further accentuated by the unusual use of the term *krt* (cut) in the description of the rushed circumcision (in Hebrew covenants are "cut": the common expression being *likhrot berit*). There is indeed a covenant in the air. But it is a blood covenant, which reconfirms the marital bond between Zipporah and her revived spouse. It is not a covenant between Yahweh and Moses. If it were, Moses would have had to be defined as Yahweh's bride, given that it is God who traditionally plays the role of bridegroom in the Bible (for a similar critique, see Kosmala 1962:25).

"The Bridegroom of Blood" would have definitely blended better in Exodus had it simply represented what Talmon forces it to represent: the "cutting" of a covenant between the Father and His chosen son. But this is not quite the case. Much that goes on in this Yahwistic text undoubtedly disrupts the monotheistic framework within which it is set.

Textual Traces

Harold Bloom defines J as an uncanny writer whose fierce and primal understanding of human personality and provocative apprehension of divine realities (1982:xiv) outshine the representations of other (belated) biblical sources. I tend to agree with Bloom's depiction of J's daring antithetical bent, although I am not terribly concerned about determining which biblical source is the strongest. What Bloom's analysis of the Yahwistic text fails to take into account is the fact that even the strikingly original Yahwist (or Yahwists) had precursors.[10] I believe that in J one often hears voices whose polytheistic character is most pronounced. What is really powerful about the Yahwistic strand is its capacity on occasion to come close to myth, allowing for the sort of tension none of the other strands can sustain.

The eeriness of "The Bridegroom of Blood" in fact stems from the closeness of elements which pertain to a repressed pagan past. To use Daniel Boyarin's (1990a:98) apt definition of another rather mythical moment in Exodus (the parting of the Red Sea), "The Bridegroom of Blood" reveals "a faultline between ideologies"; it is the site of conflict between polytheistic and monotheistic traditions.

So far I have tried to elucidate Zipporah's role during this nocturnal episode by pointing to the similarity between her daring deliverance and that of the female characters in Exodus 1–2, but the striking otherness of her struggle is no less intriguing. The triumph of the female saviors over the mighty Pharaoh in the opening chapters of Exodus is truly wondrous and astounding, but it is still far more palatable than Zipporah's uncanny victory in "The Bridegroom of Blood." Zipporah's opponent is not merely an august father figure, but the Father Himself! By warding off Yahweh, Zipporah thus endangers monotheistic tenets, as well as patriarchal ones.

Eduard Meyer (1906) and his followers have pointed out that the characterization of Yahweh in Exodus 4 has a polytheistic resonance.[11] The attacker seems far more like a demonic deity than a monotheistic God, not only because of His inexplicable desire to kill Moses but also because of the manner in which He is placated. The monotheistic God, as Kaufmann puts it in *The Religion of Israel,* unlike pagan deities, "is supreme over all. There is no realm above or beside him to limit his absolute sovereignty. He is utterly distinct from, and other than, the world; he is subject to no laws, no compulsions, or powers that transcend him" (1972:60). That is why He cannot possibly yield to someone else's will, nor to simple apotropaic tricks. One should bear in mind that the apotropaic value of circumcision was widely acknowledged in the ancient world. In the Bible, however, circumcision becomes the sign of the covenant. It is usually discussed within the context of extensive covenantal affirmations (see Gen. 17, and Exod. 12), and its apotropaic character—with the exception of our curious story—is relegated to the background (see Loewenstamm 1972:87).[12]

Let me suggest that it is not only Yahweh who bears polytheistic marks in this episode. What most biblical scholars have overlooked is that the representation of Zipporah comes strikingly close to representations of guardian goddesses in polytheistic texts. Such goddesses are frequently the primary caretakers of striving young heroes. Thus Babylonian rulers are designated as the protected "bridegrooms" of Ishtar (see Ochshorn 1988:22); in Sumerian mythology the goddess Inanna ensures the prosperity of King Dumuzi; and even in the *Odyssey* and the *Aeneid,* it is Athena and Venus who are the primary guardians and instructors of their respective protégés, Odysseus and Aeneas. What is more, the protection these goddesses offer often entails struggles with other deities (usually male deities) on behalf of their chosen heroes.

With the rise of monotheism, goddesses are dethroned. God is one and as such He is male. Divine protection is solely in male hands. Yet female guardianship does not vanish; it is transferred to the human realm and perceived as the role of female characters, of mothers in particular. What we witness in "The Bridegroom of Blood" are conspicuous traces of this cultural transaction. Zipporah is a mere human being, a mother and a wife, but in her struggle against Yahweh and in her ceremonious designation of Moses as her bridegroom she seems to play something of the role of a goddess.

The Egyptian Connection

There have been several attempts on the part of biblical scholars to seek specific polytheistic origins for "The Bridegroom of Blood." Kosmala (1962) and Morgenstern (1963) have offered Midianite solutions, but so little is known about Midianite culture that their interpretations remain highly speculative.[13] Even those (Irvin 1977; Fontaine 1988) who have chosen a more substantial path—Egyptian mythology—have focused on an unconvincing parallel between Zipporah and the bloodthirsty goddess, Hathor, problematically transferring unregulated violence from Yahweh to Zipporah.

Succumbing to the same temptation to discover the foreign origins of this tale, I would conjecture that "The Bridegroom of Blood" is a modified version of the Egyptian myth of Isis and Osiris.[14] Isis, the Egyptian savior goddess, also known as the "lady of enchantments," gained renown for her successful resurrection of her husband-brother, Osiris, and later for her saving of her son Horus. Osiris, initially the divine ruler of Egypt, was murdered by his jealous brother Seth. According to Plutarch, Seth lured Osiris to lie down in a beautiful sarcophagus, thereupon his helpers suddenly rushed in, locked the coffin, and cast it into the Nile. After intensive searching and wandering Isis obtained the coffin. Some say that Seth got hold of the body once again and dismembered it. Isis, however, managed to collect the members of Osiris' body and brought him back to life by means of magical formulas and by waving her wings (that is, providing the deceased with wind or breath). An Osiris Hymn beautifully depicts this dramatic scene:

> His sister was his guard.
> She who drives off the foes,
> Who stops the deeds of the disturber
> By the power of her utterance . . .
> Mighty Isis who protected her brother,
> Who sought him without wearying.
> Who roamed the land lamenting,
> Not resting till she found him,
> Who made a shade with her plumage,
> Created breath with her wings.
> Who jubilated, joined her brother,
> Raised the weary one's inertness [his phallus],
> Received the seed, bore the heir [Horus].[15]

The focus of the resurrection is the revivification of Osiris' phallus and the consequent impregnation of Isis. (According to another version, Isis actually uses wood as a substitute for the one member she could not find.) This is how Osiris began his career as the king of the dead, later to become a vegetation god as well.

Osiris' resurrection is depicted time and again in Egyptian art as well. Isis usually appears in human form with long wings behind the bier of the deceased. Occasionally she is represented as a hawk or a kite, hovering over the dead body (and particularly over the penis) of her husband. (See the accompanying figures.)

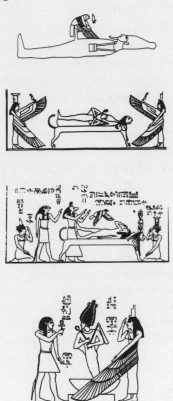

The similarities between this myth and "The Bridegroom of Blood" are fascinating! We have here a violent persecutor, a wife saving her husband, a penis undergoing treatment—perhaps the unusual use of the verb *krt* (cut) in the depiction of the circumcision in Exodus 4 echoes Osiris' dismemberment—magical formulas, and above all, wings!

Zipporah means "bird" in Hebrew, and I venture to suggest that this name discloses her affiliation with Isis.

Interestingly, Isis' drawing of Osiris out of a box in the Nile calls to mind Pharaoh's daughter.[16] But there is more. She also has much in common with Yocheved, Miriam, and the midwives (see Greenberg 1969:40; Leach 1983). The Egyptian protectress gives birth to Horus in a "papyrus thicket," where she then hides him to prevent Seth from harming the child. And because of her admirable caretaking of Horus, Isis (at times accompanied by her sister Nephthys) becomes the divine midwife of royal births. The Egyptian Pharaoh in fact was regarded as the embodiment of Horus while living, and of Osiris upon his death, being protected in both cases by the wings of Isis and her cunning magic.[17]

The similarities between the stories of Osiris and his son Horus, which are reflected in the dual personality of the Egyptian king, make better sense of the double saving of Moses—first in the ark and then at the night lodging on the way. They also may serve as a clue to the blurred demarcation between Moses and his son in Exodus 4.

God no doubt is the predominant model for saving in Exodus, but not the only one. Behind and against the Savior who freed Israel from Egypt with a "strong hand and out-stretched arm," there is a partially hidden female paradigm, whose origins, as I have suggested, may be traced back to the representation of Isis in Egyptian mythology.

In a famous passage in *Moses and Monotheism* concerning distortions caused by biblical repression of the Egyptian origins of monotheism, Freud claims that

> The distortion of a text is not unlike a murder. The difficulty lies not in the execution of the deed but in the doing away with the traces. One could wish to give the word "distortion" the double meaning to which it has a right, although it is no longer used in this sense. It should mean not only "to change the appearance of," but also "to wrench apart," "to put in another place." That is why in so many textual distortions we may

count on finding the suppressed an abnegated material hidden away somewhere, though in an altered shape and torn out of its original connection. Only it is not always easy to recognize it. (1967:52)

Although Freud was not interested in the traces left by the Egyptian savior goddess in Exodus (this seems to be the one perfect murder he attributes to Judaism), his analysis of the dynamics of repression is most appropriate in this respect. Isis is indeed "wrenched apart" as her role of midwife-mother-sister-wife is divided among Shiphrah, Puah, Yocheved, Miriam, Pharaoh's daughter, and Zipporah. If I have chosen to focus on Zipporah's story, it is because in this case the flutter of Isis' wings is far more apparent. One can clearly sense the clash between rigorous monotheistic censorship and the powerful thrust of the repressed cultural past.

The Politics of Transitions

Does the repression of goddesses in the Bible indicate that monotheism is patriarchal whereas paganism is affiliated with matriarchy? Freud, among others, adheres to such a view. In another well-known passage in *Moses and Monotheism,* he implicitly applies the ideas of J. J. Bachofen to the monotheistic revolution, defining the formation of monotheism as a progressive move which involves a transition from "maternal" values to "paternal" ones. "The progress in spirituality," Freud claims,

consists in deciding against the direct sense perception in favour of the so-called higher intellectual processes—that is to say, in favour of memories, reflection, and deduction. An example of this would be the decision that paternity is more important than maternity, although the former cannot be proved by the senses as the latter can. This is why the child has to have the father's name and inherit after him. Another example would be: our God is the greatest and mightiest, although he is invisible like the storm and the soul. (1967:150–151)

The perception of pagan tradition as bearing a matriarchal stamp also prevails in spiritual feminist writings. Thus in various anthologies such as *Womanspirit Rising* (1979), edited by Carol P. Christ and Judith Plaskow, and *The Politics of Women's Spirituality* (1982), edited by Charlene Spretnak, there is an earnest attempt to resurrect the Goddesses of the ancient world and reestablish an alternative religion whose central figure is not the authoritarian, transcendent, and abstract Father, but rather the immanent, and delightful, incarnate Mother Goddess.

Freud's association of polytheism and matriarchy is meant to highlight the spiritual advance which monotheism—with its patriarchal worldview—has brought about. Christ, Plaskow, and Spretnak attempt to do the reverse. Regardless of the obvious differences, the two approaches are equally problematic in their presentation of one sex as superior to the other, in their reliance on stereotypical gender constructions, and in their failure to consider the patriarchal bent of polytheistic religions.[18]

After all, pantheons, whether Egyptian, Babylonian, or Greek, are run by supreme male deities. Furthermore, the power of the goddesses is constricted for the most part to the fostering of their sons or male protégés. And in cases in which their power endangers male authority, they are often silenced or even murdered. Tiamat, the Great Mother of Babylonian mythology, is dismembered by Marduk (the world is built over her dead body). And even the enchanting Isis was beheaded by her son Horus (according to one tradition) or raped by him (according to another version), once the latter's rule was established.

The move away from representations of female deities in biblical texts, I contend, need not be seen as proof of the replacement of a matriarchal order (if such a thing ever existed) by a patriarchal one, but rather as an indication that the transition from paganism to monotheism entails a shift between two different patriarchal figurations of femininity. To understand this difference, one must bear in mind that the monotheistic dethroning of goddesses is part of a larger transference of drama from heaven to earth. Monotheism is turned toward humanity: theogonies are replaced by genealogies, divine struggles and intrigues turn into human affairs, demons become internal conflicts, and goddesses are humanized.[19]

The monotheistic focus on humanity is compatible with the preference of historical time over the mythical perception of time. While the episode of Isis' saving of Osiris is set in what Bakhtin calls "the absolute past" and is "walled off absolutely from all subsequent times" (1981:15), Exodus begins with a historical event that is very much connected with the present, with Pharaonic oppression and the rebellion of the Hebrew slaves. Accordingly, the female saviors in Exodus, unlike their divine precursor, have a historical role. In their daring deception of Pharaoh they get the revolution going, enable the exodus of an oppressed nation, and shape the founding scene in the history of the children of Israel.[20]

I should add, however, that the opposition between myth and history is not clear-cut. Mythologies (particularly Greek and Roman ones) rely in part on historical events, and monotheistic history is not innocent of mythical tendencies (as in its cyclical patterning of given historical phenomena).[21] The difference in emphasis, nevertheless, is significant.

Longings

And yet, just as the secular revolution has not freed its participants of sporadic longings for a monotheistic past in which faith reigned (as evident in the continual need of modern writers to allude to biblical texts, however subversive their allusions may be), so monotheism was not wholly successful in its attempt to transform or eradicate polytheistic practices. One can trace in the Bible, I think, an ineluctable attraction to the power polytheistic texts have accumulated during the thousands of years in which they were circulated.[22] No matter how powerful monotheistic substitutes and transformations of polytheistic figurations of female deities may have been, there was apparently an underlying desire for a maternal representative in the divine sphere.[23] This need is apparent not only in the prophetic depictions of the common worship of goddesses among the Israelites but also in implicit intertextual transactions in texts such as Eve's naming of Cain (Gen. 4:1), and of course in "The Bridegroom of Blood." Although I have focused on the question of goddesses, these longings are felt in other repressed pagan realms such as the demonic and the underworld (whose relevance—particularly that of the former—to the deadly attack in Exod. 4 is apparent). Interestingly, all these repressed realms were revived in rabbinic Judaism, in Kabbalah, and in Christianity—one more proof, perhaps, of their lack in biblical times and of their irrepressible power.

Monotheism, with its intense focus on one omnipotent God, had much to offer, but its very advantage embodied its drawbacks. The capacity of a male deity to play maternal roles (when necessary) wasn't always convincing. In Numbers 11, Moses, complaining as usual, asks God "Did I conceive all this people, did I bear them, that you should say unto me, 'Carry them in your bosom as a nurse carries an infant,' to the land that you have promised on oath to their fathers?" (11–12).[24]

Trible (1978: 68–69) quotes this passage to corroborate her notion that God has feminine facets which are no less important than His male traits. What she fails to notice is that Moses' rhetorical questions imply that God is quite a failure as a mother and a nurse. And if He hasn't been too successful in providing the children of Israel with the much-needed maternal care, why should His servant be capable of doing so?

Eruption

When Zipporah erupts in Exodus 4 with the power of an Isis and releases Moses from his fear of flying—by teaching him how to fly low and protecting him with her wings—she exposes one of monotheism's weak points; she lays bare a lack the Father hasn't fully managed to compensate for. The story of Isis is not all that antipatriarchal. Her tricking of a male deity is permissible within a polytheistic framework. Yet when this polytheistic text seeps into the Bible—bearing a strong aroma of its mythical origin—it becomes an antithetical element that unsettles its textual surroundings both in its antipatriarchal bent and in its anticovenantal (given the traditional notion of covenant in the Bible) spirit.

Zipporah overcomes Yahweh in this fleeting moment in which patriarchy and monotheism prove vulnerable, but then she basically disappears. The ceremonial reunion between Moses and Zipporah is immediately denied. Zipporah is mentioned once again in Exodus 18, when she is brought back to Moses by Jethro: "Then Jethro, Moses' father in law, took Zipporah, Moses' wife, after he [Moses] had sent her back" and came with her and her sons "unto Moses into the wilderness, where he encamped at the mount of God" (2–5). We are not told why Moses had sent Zipporah home, but the fact that he doesn't even greet her upon her return (he speaks only with Jethro) seems to indicate that this relationship has little meaning for him. He is now, as it were, married to God.

Zipporah's representation in Exodus, to use Erich Auerbach's (1953) wonderful expression, is "fraught with background"; it demands interpretation. I have tried to provide her with a partial background, but it would require some of Zipporah's magical powers to deliver fully a history that has been so severely curtailed.

The Book of Ruth:
Idyllic Revisionism

Perhaps the selfsame song that found a path
Through the sad heart of Ruth, when, sick for home,
She stood in tears amid the alien corn.

 —John Keats, "Ode to a Nightingale"

the book of Ruth, an idle, bungling story, foolishly
told, nobody knows by whom, about a strolling
country girl, creeping slyly to be with her cousin
Boaz. Pretty stuff indeed, to be called the Word of
God! It is however, one of the best books in the
Bible, for it is free from murder and rapine.

 —Thomas Paine, *The Age of Reason*

In the final chapter of the Book of Ruth the people at the gate
deliver the following blessing: "The Lord make the woman
that is come into thine house like Rachel and like Leah, which
two did build the house of Israel" (4:11). Abraham, Isaac, and
Jacob are often evoked to highlight the continual manifestation of divine blessing in history, but this is the only case in
the Bible where matriarchs are called up from the past to
serve as a model for the future "building"[1] of the house of
Israel.[2] The peaceful construction of a matrilineal tradition
within the framework of a blessing addressed to a would-be
father reveals an intricate mode of revisionism, which I call
"idyllic revisionism."

 For many commentators the idyllic aspects of the Book
of Ruth have served as proof of the apolitical character of the

text. Thus, B. M. Vellas criticizes the suggestion that the Book of Ruth is a polemic against the strict prohibition to marry foreign women in the period of Ezra and Nehemiah: "A book which was written in those troubled times of Ezra and Nehemiah as a protest against those men could not possess that beautiful atmosphere and those idyllic surroundings which, so skillfully, the author of Ruth creates, nor could it be possible to possess an unforced, serene and calm tone of style" (1954:7).[3] Whether or not this text was written in "those troubled times," its harmonious character does not preclude a polemical angle. Despite, or perhaps by means of, its beautiful idyllic facade, the Book of Ruth manages to challenge the biblical tendency to exclude the other (there is no need to limit oneself to Ezra and Nehemiah in this respect).[4] Such tolerance toward the stranger, however, is inextricably bound up with a more respectful approach to femininity. Ruth is, after all, doubly other—both a foreigner and a woman. As such, her honorable incorporation within the house of Israel calls for a different perception of this house and a greater recognition of its female "builders."

In its idyllic reinterpretation of the history of the founding mothers of Israel, the Book of Ruth violates a whole array of conventions, the primary one being the gender of its protagonists. If women in the Bible usually serve as a foil against which the deeds of the fathers are presented, in this narrative the subplot becomes the main plot in, as it were, a biblical parallel to Stoppard's *Rosencrantz and Guildenstern Are Dead*.[5] And as the marginal becomes central, the limitations of feminine perspectives elsewhere in biblical narrative are flaunted and challenged.

My analysis of the revisionist character of the Book of Ruth concentrates on the ways in which this text rereads the story of Leah and Rachel. To be sure, the Book of Ruth evokes numerous female characters: some explicitly and others through an implicit network of allusions. My focus on the two matriarchs is meant to correct the tendency to dwell mostly on Tamar's story in studies of the intertextual interrelations between the Book of Ruth and Genesis,[6] as well as to enable a consideration of the re-presentation of relations between women in a text whose perception of the other is so different.

The Plot of Female Bonding

In a reversal of the traditional hierarchy of male and female plots, the central plot of the Book of Ruth is a female one. And as is often the case in biblical narrative, the main plot precedes the subplot. The Book of Ruth opens with a strikingly feminine chapter (the only men mentioned are dead) in which the protagonists, Ruth and Naomi, are introduced. Whereas in Genesis the plot is concerned mainly with Jacob's well-being, and the deeds of Leah and Rachel are seen in relation to their husband's needs, here, from the very outset, the problems of Ruth and Naomi—widowhood, childlessness, lack of economic means, and estrangement—are placed at the center; so much so that they enter into the public domain as Naomi depicts her state of misery to the women of Bethlehem. But what does this foregrounding of what elsewhere would be the subplot reveal about relations between women?

The allusion to the two matriarchs in the Book of Ruth may serve as a clue. The two notorious rivals seem to share the same roof in exemplary harmony: "The Lord make the woman that is come into thine house like Rachel and like Leah, which two did build the house of Israel." To use Harold Bloom's revisionary ratios, the idyllic revisionism of the Book of Ruth comes closest to *tessera*. According to Bloom, "A poet antithetically 'completes' his precursor, by so reading the parent-poem as to retain its terms but to mean them in another sense, as though the precursor had failed to go far enough" (1973:14). Bloom takes the term from Jacques Lacan, "whose own revisionary relationship to Freud might be given as an instance of *tessera*" (p. 67). The context in which the term originates, however, is the early mystery religions, where fitting together again the two halves of a broken piece of pottery was used as a means of recognition, a password of sorts, by the initiates.[7]

On the face of it, there is no apparent aggression toward Genesis ("the parent-text") in the above-mentioned blessing. Ruth merely seems to be following in the footsteps of her female precursors. Like Leah and Rachel, she too serves principal patriarchal values such as the preservation of line and the return to the Promised Land. And yet, within this patriarchal framework, the Book of Ruth offers an antithetical "completion" of the limited representation of female bonding in Genesis. In evoking Leah and Rachel as the two *cobuilders* of the house of Israel, the Book of Ruth both highlights the brief moments in which the two matriarchs manage to cooperate and calls into question the emphasis put on rivalry in the story of Leah and Rachel as well as in the scarce representations of relationships between women elsewhere in biblical narrative.

In *A Room of One's Own,* Virginia Woolf expresses a similar critique as she reads a new novel by a modern woman writer.

> "Chloe liked Olivia," I read. And then it struck me how immense a change was there. Chloe liked Olivia perhaps for the first time in literature. Cleopatra did not like Octavia. And how completely *Antony and Cleopatra* would have been altered had she done so! As it is, I thought . . . the whole thing is simplified, conventionalised, if one dared say it, absurdly. Cleopatra's only feeling about Octavia is one of jealousy. Is she taller than I am? How does she do her hair? The play, perhaps, required no more. But how interesting it would have been if

the relationship between the two women had been more complicated.   (1929:86)

The Book of Ruth is the only biblical text in which the
word "love" is used to define a relationship between two
women. And once such love is represented, an intriguing
rewriting of Genesis takes place.

From the very opening of the Book of Ruth, "clinging"
between women determines the movement of the plot.
Rejecting the option of returning to Moab to seek a new husband, Ruth chooses to "cling" (1:15) to her mother-in-law
and go wherever she goes. The verb *dbq* (cling) first appears
in Genesis 2:24 in the etiological comment which follows the
depiction of woman's creation out of *adam*'s body. "Therefore
shall a man leave his father and mother, and shall cleave [*dbq*]
unto his wife: and they shall be one flesh." "To cling" in this
case means to recapture a primal unity, to return to a time
when man and woman were literally "one flesh." That Ruth's
cleaving unto Naomi evokes Genesis 2:24 becomes more evident in Boaz's praising of Ruth's move: "It hath fully been
shewed me, all that thou hast done unto thy mother in law
since the death of thine husband: and how thou hast left thy
father and thy mother, and the land of thy nativity, and art
come unto a people which thou knewest not heretofore"
(2:11). "To leave [one's] father and mother" is the recurrent
phrase that links the two texts. Yet, while in Genesis such
leaving and cleaving defines the institution of marriage, in the
Book of Ruth it depicts female bonding, a hitherto unrecog-
nized tie.

Ruth's clinging to Naomi makes clear that rivalry is
not necessarily a predominant feature in relations between
women, even in types of relations which are particularly
prone to conflict. We are not dealing here with two cowives,
but the relationship of the mother-in-law and the daughter-
in-law is, in psychoanalytic terms, similar. The mother, after

all, is the son's first object of love. Thus even when the son marries "an outside object," the primary oedipal drama is not over. What this means for the women involved is a delicate situation in which they must share the same man. That the relationship of the mother-in-law and the daughter-in-law, as a result, may be painfully tense is all too well-known. The mother, "abandoned" by her son, is likely to be hostile toward the young woman who has replaced her, while the daughter-in-law, in turn, may try to ensure her position in her husband's heart by challenging the influence of her precursor.[8]

Struggles between fathers-in-law and sons-in-law, which usually end with the victory of the young hero, are common in biblical narrative (those of Laban and Jacob or Saul and David, for example) and could serve as a clue as to how the analogous relationship between the mother-in-law and the daughter-in-law might have been presented. In light of Freud's family romance, one could define such plots as wishful inversions of the child's failure in the initial oedipal triangle. The Book of Ruth, however, chooses to dwell on another possible development of relations with in-laws. In this text the parental in-law figure turns out to be an appropriate recipient not of hostility, but of love.[9]

The representation of triangular dynamics in this text is indeed strikingly unconventional. Of course we know nothing about the triangle of Naomi-Machlon-Ruth, but the representation of the ties of Naomi-Ruth-Boaz reveals a significant break from the traditional scene where two women compete for the same man. We find here, as in Dora's case, the resurgence of the preoedipal triangular structure in which the privileged term is not the all-powerful father, but an adored mother.[10] What the Book of Ruth thus completes in its rewriting of Genesis is the possible impact of the preoedipal phase on women's relations.

When Ruth cleaves unto Naomi, merging with her on

all possible levels—"for whither thou goest, I will go; and
where thou lodgest, I will lodge: thy people shall be my people, and thy God my God. Where thou diest, will I die, and
there will I be buried" (Ruth 1:16–17)—she may be yearning
(perhaps not unlike man in Gen. 2:24) to recapture the primal
unity with the mother, to return to an archaic moment in
which the infant and the mother are "one flesh." "Clinging,"
after all, connotes a primary mode of contact, one which precedes the more conscious and sexualized "knowing" in
Genesis 3–4 (see Gurevich 1990).

Both Boaz and Naomi call Ruth "my daughter" (a textual proof of their respective roles as parental figures), but
Ruth's attachment to her mother-in-law predominates
throughout the story. In fact, in a reversal of the patriarchal
mode of exchange where women mediate the relationship
between men, here Boaz, being a redeemer, plays the role of
the mediator, enabling not only the "resurrection" of
Machlon's name but also the preservation of the tie between
Ruth and Naomi.[11] If Ruth prefers Boaz to the *ne'arim* (young
men), it is, I think, precisely because he is a man who could,
albeit differently, "spread his wings" over both women.

Naomi never actually meets Boaz in the text, let alone
lies with him, yet her meticulous planning of Ruth's seductive moves at the threshing floor makes her a vicarious par-
ticipant in this scene. "Wash thyself," she instructs Ruth, "and
anoint thee, and put thy raiment upon thee, and get thee
down to the floor: but make not thyself known unto the man,
until he shall have done eating and drinking. And it shall be,
when he lieth down, that thou shalt mark the place where he
shall lie, and thou shalt go in, and uncover his feet, and lay
thee down; and he will tell thee what thou shalt do" (3:3–4).
The recurrent use of the first person instead of the third person in the *ketib* (Naomi says "I will go down" instead of "you
will go down" and, more significantly, "I will lie" instead of
"you will lie")—which some scholars define as an archaic

form of second-person feminine singular (see Sasson 1979: 68)—might also be considered as a slip which accentuates Naomi's vicarious involvement in this seduction or, rather, her sympathetic identification with her daughter-in-law. Ruth, for her part, makes sure that her mother-in-law does not feel left out; she rushes back to Naomi at dawn to share the barley and the experience with her. "And when she came to her mother in law . . . she told her all that the man had done to her. And she said, These six measures of barley gave he me; for he said to me, Go not empty unto thy mother in law" (3:16–17).

Naomi, who claims in the beginning of the story to be "too old to have an husband" (although she imagines such a possibility: "if I should say, I have hope, if I should have an husband also to night, and should also bear sons; Would ye tarry for them till they were grown?" [1:12]), thus partially fulfills her desire through her proxy, Ruth.

Hence, as the Book of Ruth revises the story of Rachel and Leah, the rivalry between the younger and the elder co-wives gives way to a harmonious sharing of the same man. Such sharing, however, is not wholly foreign to the two matriarchs. The story of the mandrakes (Gen. 30:14–16), in which Rachel sends Leah to lie with Jacob, may be seen as a brief prefiguration of what becomes full-fledged female coop-eration in the Book of Ruth. Put differently, the momentary change in triangular dynamics which takes place in Genesis 30 becomes a continual moment in the Book of Ruth. Accordingly, the harvest season, which in Genesis defines but a brief truce in the history of Rachel and Leah, turns out to be the one and only season in the Book of Ruth. That this season is the season of fertility points to another issue the two texts share in common: "the building of the house of Israel."

The deal between the sisters, as we have seen, also involves a more equal distribution of fertility. With the help of the mandrakes Leah gives Rachel in exchange for a night with Jacob, the latter finally conceives. Here too the *tessera* is at work. The traditional split between the barren woman and the fertile one is more fully undone.[12] Both Ruth and Naomi are childless in the opening, just as both share mothering at the end. Ruth is Obed's biological mother, but Naomi takes on a maternal role as she holds the child to her bosom and becomes his nurse. That shared parenthood is at stake is made clear by the most scandalous verse in this text: "A son is born to Naomi." This is a radical violation of the formula according to which the son is born to the father. To give but two examples, "And to Seth . . . there was born a son" (Gen. 4:26); "These are the sons of Rachel, which were born to Jacob" (Gen. 46:22). Interestingly, both Rachel and Sarah attempt to "be built" through their maids, Bilhah and Hagar. But in Genesis such vicarious maternity does not suffice; not only because of class difference (in fact one could argue that Naomi is of higher social status in Bethlehem than Ruth), but also because a different perception of female bonding is a prerequisite for a more heterogenous treatment of motherhood.

Perhaps as a way of assuring the joint motherhood of Ruth and Naomi, neither of them names the child. It is the women of Bethlehem who, in a collective female voice, give him the name "Obed."

One may well wonder why the plot of female bonding is the plot of fertility. This somewhat paradoxical combination calls to mind the myth of Demeter and her daughter Persephone. The story of the two goddesses is well known: While playing in a field of flowers with the daughters of Oceanus, Persephone is abducted by Hades, lord of the underworld. Beset by agony, Demeter goes to Eleusis to search for her. During the following year Demeter, still in mourning, revenges herself for the loss of her daughter by forbidding the grain to grow. Zeus intervenes and demands that Hades let Persephone go. Hades feigns wholehearted obedience, but he secretly gives Persephone a tiny pomegranate seed to eat, knowing that this will force her to return to the underworld for four months every year. Demeter springs annually to meet her daughter, and upon their happy reunion restores fecundity to the land. Interestingly, this is the only Greek myth which deals with the mother-daughter bond, allowing it to maintain a pivotal position in the triangle of Persephone-Demeter-Hades (so clearly represented in the ratio of the months Persephone stays with Hades vs. those spent with Demeter).

What I think is at stake in both cases—and I am not suggesting that there is necessarily a historical link between the two texts (the differences are unmistakable)—is male awe concerning female bonding and a reassurance that such bonding need not necessarily hinder the continuation of the line or the growth of grain. Ironically—and this is perhaps the greatest Eleusinian mystery—quite the contrary is true.

The Doubling of the Female Subject

Let us return to the blessing in Ruth 4:11 and ask another question: Why does Rachel appear before Leah? Does this mean that the Book of Ruth is Rachel's wish-fulfillment dream, a text in which the younger female character gains full access to heroism? That the text bears Ruth's name seems to point in this direction. Her position as the primary model in the mirroring of the female and male plots is another important factor. Boaz turns out to be Ruth's counterpart when, unlike Ploni Almoni (the Hebrew equivalent of John Doe), he chooses the unconventional way—to marry a Moabite. In so doing, he follows Ruth's exemplary act of *hesed* (kindness) toward Naomi, which is set against the more conventional decision of Orpah.[13] In fact, the extent to which dreams are fulfilled in the Book of Ruth needs to be seen as yet another aspect of its revisionism, for the Hebrew Bible, as we have seen, tends to deny fulfillment, particularly when female dreams are at stake.

The intimate bond between Ruth and Naomi, however, interrupts this symmetrical mirroring and fosters a rare construction of heroism. In a strange way Ruth and Naomi manage to share not only a husband and a son, but also textual subjectivity. Though differently, both in a sense fulfill Rachel's dream. Insofar as the romantic plot is concerned, Ruth is in the position of the young male hero whose desires determine the movement of the plot (see Brooks 1984: 90–112). Yet Naomi has an equally important narratological role since she is the one who undergoes a significant inner transformation in the course of the story. Despite her limited textual life span (we get to know her only as an aged woman), she is "fraught with development," in Auerbach's terms, to a degree no other female character in the Bible reaches.

In the opening chapter of the Book of Ruth we encounter a bitter, mournful, childless, and angry widow, accusing God of afflicting her with such "emptiness": "And she said unto them, Call me not Naomi, call me Mara: for the Almighty hath dealt very bitterly [*hemar*] with me. I went out full, and the Lord hath brought me home again empty: why then call ye me Naomi, seeing the Lord hath testified against me, and the Almighty hath afflicted me?" (1:20–21). One hears in Naomi's voice the same acute pain which is evident in Rachel's cry: "Give me children or else I die" (Gen. 30:1). Childlessness is synonymous with death. What the Book of Ruth adds, however, to the portrait of the barren one is a Jobian protest. As Campbell points out, Naomi, not unlike Job, "portrays herself as defendant in a legal action in which the charges and the testimony are in effect unknown to her . . . in which the punishment has already been meted out" (1975:83). Already in Rachel's first naming-speech, one finds a reference to a kind of trial before God regarding barrenness:

"God hath judged me, and hath also heard my voice, and hath given me a son: therefore called she his name Dan" (Gen. 30:6). But it requires a text in which women are protagonists and naming-speeches serve as an explicit mode of female self-characterization—"Call me not Naomi [a derivation of "pleasant" or "sweet"], call me Mara" ["the bitter one"]—to take God to task for the childlessness he inflicts on women with no apparent justification. As in the case of Job, by struggling against the ruthless "hand of God," Naomi attains a loftier position vis-à-vis God, which is synonymous with attaining a greater narratological role.

God does not respond out of a whirlwind, but then he is not really a character in the Book of Ruth. As Campbell puts it, "God's activity in the Ruth Book is very much that of one in the shadows" (1975:28), one whose power is manifested by means of human agents. In accordance with such "humanist" theology, Naomi's faith is restored through a growing realization that divine *hesed* is revealed through human *hesed*. "Blessed be he of the Lord, who hath not left off his kindness [*hesed*] to the living and to the dead" (2:20), says Naomi, upon hearing about Boaz's kindness toward Ruth during their first encounter in the field. She now realizes that God hasn't deserted (*'azv*) her and that, with some spurring, Boaz, the redeemer, can play the role of *the* Redeemer. (The verb "to redeem" is surely more than a legalistic term in this text.) Ruth will deliver this message to Boaz at the threshing floor, when asking him to spread his wings over her, urging him to do what he previously assigned to God (2:12).

What Naomi further realizes at this turning point is that she herself can become an agent of divine *hesed*. If in 1:9 she evokes the Lord as the one who will provide her daughters-in-law with "rest," now she herself takes the initiative in this respect: "Then Naomi her mother in law said unto her, My daughter, shall I not seek rest for thee, that it may be well with thee? And now is not Boaz of our kindred . . . Behold, he winnoweth barley to night in the threshingfloor. Wash thyself therefore" (3:1–3).

Naomi's changed attitude toward God is inseparable from a transformation in her relationship with Ruth. Initially Naomi's mourning, which verges on melancholia,[14] does not allow her to acknowledge the value of Ruth's *hesed,* nor to believe that she is worthy of receiving such *hesed.* Ruth's ardent oath of loyalty is never reciprocated. Naomi remains silent. Similarly, in her bleak complaint to the women of Bethlehem, Naomi will still describe herself as old and empty, ignoring Ruth's clinging to her.

But when Ruth returns from Boaz's field with the good news, Naomi speaks to her for the first time in the first-person plural, referring to Boaz as one of *"our* redeemers." If the matriarchs in Genesis are busy scheming against fathers so that their favorite sons will be heirs, here we have a unique case where a woman struggles for the well-being and inheritance of another woman. Naomi discovers that, unexpectedly, mothering a daughter-in-law may be rewarding as well.

The story ends with a fuller Naomi, clasping a child to her bosom. We do not have direct access to her feelings, but the female "chorus" of the women of Bethlehem seems to serve as a mirror which reflects Naomi's happiness. "And the women said unto Naomi, Blessed be the Lord, which hath not left thee this day without a kinsman, that his name may be famous in Israel. And he shall be unto thee a restorer of thy life, and a nourisher of thine old age: for thy daughter in law, which loveth thee, which is better to thee than seven sons, hath born him" (4:14–15). The women provide a blessing of God, a thanksgiving, which intimates that now that the Redeemer has fulfilled his role and has provided Naomi with a "restorer of life," a full reconciliation between Naomi and God can take place. The trial has come to an end.

Here too the restoration of faith in God is inextricably

linked to an ability to believe in an unconventional bond: "For thy daughter in law, which loveth thee . . . is better to thee than seven sons" (4:15). "What more appropriate way," writes Campbell, "to praise Ruth than to say she is worth seven times what the story has made such an absorbing concern—a son!" (1975:168). Naomi, so it seems, was "full" from the very beginning (Ruth being at her side) without realizing it. Little wonder that the chorus' radical statement appears only after the birth of a son.

The change in Naomi is analogous to the transition from bitterness and humiliation to happiness and restoration of faith in the annunciation type-scene. Sarah's skeptical laughter (upon hearing the annunciation) turns into a poetic celebration of her miraculous conception: "And Sarah said, God hath made me to laugh, so that all that hear will laugh with me. And she said, Who would have said unto Abraham, that Sarah should have given children suck? for I have born him a son in his old age" (Gen. 21:6–7). Similarly, Rachel's despair and lack of faith give way to a happy name-giving (Gen. 30:23). And Hannah, who first defines herself as a woman "bitter in the soul," turns into a happy mother. Her Song is a homage to God's transformative powers: "so that the barren hath born seven; and she that hath many children is waxed feeble" (1 Sam. 2:5).

What makes Naomi's case different is not only the development of a Jobian protest and the valorization of female bonding, but also the fact that her inner transformation does not stem from bodily alteration. Her rhetorical question in 1:12 may give rise at first to expectations that, like Sarah, she will miraculously give birth to a son in her old age, but as the text unfolds a different perception of mothering and faith emerges, calling into question the limited representation of nonbodily changes in the annunciation type-scene. God indeed leaves traces on the bodies of his male elects as well, but such traces are secondary in relation to the spiritual changes which accompany them. (Thus more emphasis is put on Jacob's change of name than on the mark left on his thigh.)

The Book of Ruth, with its doubling of the female subject, offers a split annunciation type-scene and thus a critique of the intense embodiedness of the barren one.[15] I do not mean to suggest that Naomi's transformation could have happened without the substantiation of divine providence through the impregnation of Ruth. Nevertheless, this text provides a division between "body" and "voice" which defies the stereotypical attribution of the former primarily to woman and the latter primarily to man.[16]

Estrangement

One more transformation is at stake: the transition from estrangement to rootedness. The passage which most clearly touches upon this issue in Genesis is the encounter in the field (31:5–17), where the two sisters, with one voice, define their status in Laban's household as that of *nokhriyot* (foreign women), expressing willingness to follow Jacob to his land. The order of presentation—Rachel before Leah—in the blessing of the people at the gate may in fact be perceived, among other things, as a marker meant to enhance the intertextual interaction between the two texts. (As we have seen, this is the only occasion in Genesis where the sisters are mentioned in this order.)

Here once again we witness a division of roles between Ruth and Naomi which allows for an interplay between the literal and figurative expressions of a given phenomenon. Ruth is the official stranger, the one who has "come unto a people which [she] knewest not heretofore" (2:11). Naomi's self-estrangement, however, complements the foreignness of her daughter-in-law. "Is this Naomi?" ask the women of Bethlehem with one voice as they enter the city. Even if the "female chorus" simply finds it hard to recognize Naomi after all these years, their question reflects her inner state of turmoil and alienation. In response to their question she says: "Call me not Naomi, Call me Mara: for the Almighty hath dealt very bitterly with me. I went out full, and the Lord hath brought me home again empty" (1:20–21).

I have previously analyzed these verses in dealing with Naomi's bitter complaint about widowhood and, above all, childlessness. Now I would like to add a third source of bitterness, one clearly related to the former two: estrangement. One should bear in mind that the term for "barren" in Hebrew, *'aqara,* literally means "uprooted," which is why the barren one serves as a symbolic representation for the exiled nation in prophetic texts (for example, Isa. 54:1–3).[17]

Naomi underscores her inner alienation by pointing out the emptiness of her name, the primary marker of identity. "Naomi" no longer suits her, she claims, suggesting that a more appropriate name would be "Mara," the bitter one. What makes things worse is that her home, like her name, is estranged. There is nothing more alienating and unheroic than returning to one's home empty-handed. Male protagonists—Jacob is a fine example—make sure they return home with wives, children, and a good deal of property. (In the national return from Egypt this will be defined as leaving *birekhush gadol,* with great substance.) Homecoming, the touchstone of heroism in biblical narrative as well as in other ancient texts, is far more difficult when a woman takes on such a task. Naomi returns to Judea with no divine promise, without a husband, with no sons, and without a penny to her name. Her return, at least in the initial stages, turns out to be worse than exile, for she feels, not unlike Rachel and Leah, a stranger in her own homeland.

As the text unfolds, however, the acute sense of estrangement is gradually alleviated. Ruth is the first to experience the change. In the first encounter between Ruth and

Boaz in the field he calls Ruth *bitti* (my daughter) and offers
her unlimited gleaning in his field. She responds with a
question: "Why have I found grace in thine eyes, that
thou shouldst take knowledge of me, seeing I am a stranger?"
(2:10). Ruth's pun—*lehakir* (take knowledge) and *nokhriya*
(stranger) share the same root: *nkhr*—is meant to accentuate
the surprisingly different approach toward the other in this
text. Playing the role of the devil's advocate, Ruth raises the
question opponents of such tolerance are bound to ask, giving Boaz a chance to respond with a challenge to the predominant tendency to "make oneself a stranger" *(lehitnaker)* in
relation to a foreigner instead of "recognizing" *(lehakir)* him
or her.

Ruth will still manage to startle Boaz during their second
encounter at the threshing floor (3:8), but this sudden erup-
tion of xenophobia cannot but yield to the idyllic mood of
the text. Boaz finally recovers from the shock and acknowledges the gift, or rather the *hesed,* Ruth has offered him.
His determination to marry her is so strong from this point
on that even the reluctance of Ploni Almoni about marry-
ing Ruth (probably because of her Moabite origin) cannot
shatter it.

The Book of Ruth, to quote the blessing in 4:11 once
again, ends with the incorporation of Ruth the Moabite
within Boaz's house. "House," one of the key words in this
text, thus acquires a different meaning. Bethlehem, the
"house of bread," which had little to offer Ruth and Naomi
when they first arrived in the city, turns out to be more hos-
pitable once they have become part of Boaz's household.

That Naomi finally finds her way back home is also inti-
mated by the sudden emergence of her piece of land in 4:3.
The deferred emergence of Naomi's lot has long perplexed
commentators who have not taken the figurative implications
of this event into consideration. Just as the absence of this

piece of land up until this point coincides with Naomi's initial sense of homelessness, so its appearance in the happy ending reveals the change in Naomi's feelings toward Judea.

Rachel and Leah follow Jacob to Canaan with the implied hope that in that foreign land they will feel more at home than in their father's household. But upon their arrival in the Promised Land, both vanish from the scene. We never learn whether or not their move into the house of Israel brought about a change in their sense of estrangement. Rachel's death on the way to Bethlehem may in fact point to the contrary.

The Book of Ruth begins where the story of Rachel ends: on the way to Bethlehem, between two lands, in a double exile. It focuses, however, on the familiarization of estranged women within the Land of Israel. In what may be defined once again as a double fulfillment of Rachel's dream, both Naomi and Ruth take root in Bethlehem; both are ancestresses of David.

But the matter is somewhat more complicated, for as the estranged becomes familiar, the familiar is defamiliarized. The Book of Ruth inserts the other at the very root of the royal line. Ruth assimilates within the House of Israel, but remains "Ruth the Moabite" until the very end.

The Book of Ruth, as Julia Kristeva would have it, does not encourage deviance nor proselytism; instead it invites us "to consider the fertility of the other" (1991:75). It maintains, in other words, a delicate balance between same and other, where the other, through its very otherness, "builds" the House of Israel.

A Midrashic Parallel

A beautiful midrash in Lamentations Rabba about Rachel and Leah may help to sum up the revisionist aspects of the Book of Ruth through its more direct mode of rewriting. It opens with the futile attempts of Abraham, Isaac, Jacob, and Moses to persuade God to redeem His people. Finally,

> the matriarch Rachel broke forth into speech before the Holy One, blessed be He, and said, "Sovereign of the Universe, it is revealed before Thee that Thy servant Jacob loved me exceedingly and toiled for my father on my behalf seven years. When those seven years were completed and the time arrived for my marriage with my husband, my father planned to substitute another for me and to wed my husband for the sake of my sister. It was very hard for me, because the plot was known to me and I disclosed it to my husband; and I gave him a sign whereby he could distinguish between me and my sister, so that my father should not be able to make the substitution. After that I relented, suppressed my desire, and had pity upon my sister that she should not be exposed to shame. In the evening they substituted my sister for me with my husband, and I delivered over to my sister all the signs which I had arranged with my husband . . . More than that, I went beneath the bed upon which he lay with my sister; and when he spoke to her she remained silent and I made all the replies in order that he should not recognize my sister's voice. I did her a kindness *(hesed)*, was not jealous of her, and did not expose her to shame. And if I, a creature of flesh and blood, formed of dust and ashes, was not envious of my rival . . . why shouldest Thou, a King Who liveth eternally and are merciful, be jealous of idolatry in which there is no reality, and exile my children and let them be slain by the sword, and their enemies have done with them as they wished!"
>
> Forthwith the mercy of the Holy One, blessed be He, was stirred, and He said, "For thy sake, Rachel, I will restore Israel to their place." And so it is written . . . *A voice is heard in Ramah.*[18]

This provocative midrash, like the Book of Ruth, harmonizes the relationship between Rachel and Leah. Rivalry is replaced by love and *hesed,* and competition over husband turns into exemplary sharing. Here too a vicarious seduction is at work. The midrashic Rachel is a little more daring than Naomi. She actually lies beneath the nuptial bed of Jacob and Leah and supplements her sister's physical motions with the appropriate sounds. Here too one finds a challenge to patriarchal order and a complaint about divine injustice. Rachel "breaks forth" (literally, "jumps," *kaftsa*) without being called up, and boldly criticizes God for being irrationally jealous of idolatry to the extent of inflicting excessive punishments on His people. In a fascinating move she turns jealousy from a female issue into a divine one. Interestingly, it is Rachel's insolent rebuke—and not the words of the patriarchs, nor even the plea of the great Moses—which brings about a change in the course of events, "stirring" the Father. God, like Boaz, needs to be spurred on to redeeming by an other. Here too, then, the antithetical completion of female bonding and initiative turns out to be unexpectedly essential to the prosperity of the House of Israel.

❦ 7 ❧

"I Am a Wall, and My Breasts like Towers": The Song of Songs and the Question of Canonization

The inclusion of the Song of Songs within the Holy Scriptures never ceases to perplex modern readers. The features most often presented as incompatible with the biblical worldview are: the conspicuous absence of God; the lack of national themes; and the daring erotic character of the dialogue between the two lovers. Following Phyllis Trible, I would like to add another deviant feature which complicates the matter even further: the Song's antipatriarchal bent. Trible defines the relationship of the lovers in the Song as an egalitarian one: "There is no male dominance, no female subordination, and no stereotyping of either sex" (1978:161). She goes on to suggest that the Song sets out to correct the patriarchal model which was established in another garden, the Garden of Eden. "Thy desire shall be to thy husband, and he shall rule over thee" is the divine judgment upon the women in Genesis 3:16. Conversely, in the Song desire relies on mutuality. Time and again the Shulamite claims "My beloved is mine and I am his." And, as if to reinforce such mutuality, there is at times a metaphoric fluidity whereby the lovers use the same vehicles to depict one another in their cocourting. Trible mentions only animal imagery (thus both are portrayed as having "dovelike eyes"—4:1; 5:12), but the lovers equally draw from other semantic fields such as flora and architecture in their eager attempts to represent each other's body.

The antipatriarchal bent of the Song is further revealed, claims Trible, in the emphasis placed on female voices. The Shulamite is the main focalizer: it is primarily her yearnings and dreams that we follow throughout the Song. Her voice is the one that leads us into the amorous dialogue, and she is the one who concludes the Song. What is more, her love is captured not only in her dialogue with her beloved but also through an ongoing exchange with a female collective voice, the voice of the daughters of Jerusalem.

Trible's perception of the Song as a text with no tensions, as a harmonic "depatriarchalized" rendition of the Garden of Eden, is somewhat problematic—as I shall soon attempt to show—but the main thrust of her argument is most convincing: the Song does indeed deviate from conventional representations of love in the Bible.

The (Im)purity of the Song

How then was such an antithetical text canonized? Were the canon-makers blind to its deviant features? We know very little about the canonization of biblical texts. The final fixing of the Holy Scriptures presumably took place sometime between the first and second centuries C.E., as part of the development of rabbinic Judaism.[1] The rabbis, however, provide no systematic account of the closing of the canon. One finds only sparse evidence concerning rabbinic disputes over the canonicity of texts such as Ecclesiastes, Esther, Ruth, and the Song of Songs.[2]

Let me suggest that the very fact that there was rabbinic debate at all about the Song's status and that of other disputable texts indicates that their otherness did not go unnoticed. The content of the debate, however, is usually less revealing. In the case of the Song, for instance, the rabbis do not spell out its antithetical aspects, nor do they explicitly refer to any set of official criteria regarding canonicity. What they are concerned with are halakhic issues. The question at stake is whether or not the Song has the power "to defile the hands" *(metame 'et hayadayim)*. According to rabbinic enactment, hands that come into contact with a biblical book contract uncleanness in the second degree. Such impurity needs to be removed by means of a ritual washing of the hands.[3] The rabbinic perception of a canonical text as a text which causes pollution is not as paradoxical as it may seem. What it determines is a special mode of circulation. Sacred texts must be handled differently.[4] Their very authority is inscribed in their capacity to affect the body of those who touch them, which is why to this very day Torah scrolls are not touched directly. (A pointer or the edge of a prayer shawl serve as means of mediation between the reader's body and the scroll.)

The great advocate of the Song was Rabbi Akiva. In an often quoted passage he defends the sacredness of the text and denies that its "impurity" was ever disputed or can be disputed. "Heaven forbid," says Rabbi Akiva, "that any man in Israel ever disputed that the Song of Songs renders the hands unclean, for the whole world is not worth the day on which the Song of Songs was given to Israel, for all the Writings are holy, and the Song of Songs is the Holy of Holies" (Mishnah Yadayim 3.5).

In a striking rhetorical move Rabbi Akiva plays with the superlative structure of the phrase Song of Songs *(shir hashirim)* and turns the text whose holiness was called into question into none other than the "Holy of Holies" *(kodesh hakodashim)*. With the same zeal, however, he sets out to limit the circulation of the Song to religious practice, as befits a canonical text.[5] "He who trills his voice in chanting the Song of Songs in the banquet house," Rabbi Akiva claims, "and treats it as a sort of song [*zemer*] has no part in the world to come."[6]

But why did Rabbi Akiva's approach prevail? Why was his definition of the Song as a binding text accepted? Most scholars attribute Akiva's success to his implicit empowering of the allegorical reading of the Song. Once the amorous dialogue between the lovers in the Song is regarded as a representation of the consecrated love between God and Israel, that is, as an extension of the prophetic metaphor concerning the covenental bond, the Song may in fact be considered as the "Holy of Holies." This argument, however, too easily irons out the unconventional features of the text. As Gerson D. Cohen claims, "The problem is, really, why anyone should have thought of treating the work as an allegory in the first place. There must have been works aplenty that were excluded from the canon and that were not reinterpreted. One must, therefore, ask why the scales were tipped in favor of this particular poem that was *a priori* so religiously questionable" (1966:3).

The traditional perception of canon-formation as a unifying process which eliminated or smoothed over contradictions—a perception that has been recently reformulated by canonical criticism—overlooks the fascinating diversity of discourses in the Bible.[7] The formation of the Hebrew canon involves not only a concern for unity, for the blending of different traditions into a unified whole; it equally entails a "respect for friction," in Geoffrey Hartman's (1986:13) terms, a respect for different truth claims, which is why religiously questionable texts such as the Song and Ecclesiastes could be canonized alongside mainstream works. Accordingly, I do not wish to refute the intertextual ties between the Song and the Prophets, but rather to point to the friction brought about once these texts are placed in the same corpus.

Whether consciously or not, whether willingly or despite themselves, the canon-makers gave expression, however limited, to voices which negated the uniformity of religious practice, to discourses which toppled sacred hierarchies. This does not mean that such antithetical elements were innocent of the marks of censorship, nor that their challenge to predominant biblical tenets was not, at least partially, appropriated to invigorate the overriding monotheistic-patriarchal discourse in the Bible.

The Bible is, in a sense, a paradigmatic case of a Bakhtinian heteroglot text, in which centripetal and centrifugal forces clash with great force. Bakhtin's depiction of the processes of centralization and decentralization in novels (his exemplary heteroglot genre) thus may shed light on biblical heteroglossia.

> The prose writer as a novelist does not strip away the intentions of others from the heteroglot language of his works, he does not violate those socio-ideological cultural horizons . . . that open up behind heteroglot languages—rather, he welcomes them into his work. The prose writer makes use of words that are already populated with the social intentions of others and compels them to serve his own intentions . . . Therefore the intentions of the prose writer are refracted, and refracted *at different angles,* depending on the degree to which the refracted, heteroglot languages he deals with are socio-ideologically alien, already embodied and already objectivized.   (1981:299–300)

Similarly, the formation of the Hebrew Bible involved both an admission of heteroglossia and a yoking of diverse socio-ideological horizons to the intentions of the redactor(s). Friction was as necessary as refraction.

Eros

To understand why the Song attained a canonical status we must consider not only the ways its otherness was mitigated once it was included in Holy Writ but also the attractive aspects of its socio-ideological alterity. I will leave the anti-patriarchal aspect of the Song pending a bit longer and turn to the most conspicuous attraction this text offers: its celebration of Eros.

While sexual rites were carried out throughout the ancient Near East, in temples and sacred groves, monotheism firmly rejected such religious practices. Obviously the radical anthropomorphic premises of ceremonies of this sort were repulsive to the monotheistic mind. I am using the word "radical" in order to make clear that anthropomorphism is not absent in the characterization of the monotheistic God, merely constrained. Yahweh does not lack a body, as is often assumed—He "walks in the garden," "smells" the sacrifices, He even reveals Himself at Mount Sinai, and more relevantly, He is male—but the biblical representations of His embodiedness are never too elaborate or graphic. Accordingly the concrete realization of His anthropomorphic traits in religious practice is absolutely forbidden.[8] This is clearly manifested in the prohibition regarding sacred prostitution: "No Israelite woman shall be a cult prostitute, nor shall any Israelite man be a cult prostitute. You shall not bring the fee of a whore or the pay of a dog [a male prostitute] into the house of the Lord your God in fulfillment of any vow, for both are abhorrent to the Lord your God" (Deut. 23:17–18, new JPS translation).

Seeing God is problematic enough—which is why it is limited to very special occasions: His climactic revelation before the nation at Mount Sinai and His "face to face" dialogues with Moses—but sleeping with God, or enacting such an event, is far too "abhorrent" even to consider.

Erotic power, however, is too great a power to eliminate altogether from the realm of faith. Even the prophets, who set out to rid the nation of pagan customs, couldn't resist appropriating sexual desire, developing it, and returning it to their audience in a different form. In fact, the prophetic representation of the conjugal relationship between God and

Israel (whose roots lie in the Pentateuch: "And thou shalt love
the Lord thy God with all thine heart, and with all thy soul,
and with all thy might" [Deut. 6:5])[9] has often been construed
as a monotheistic transformation of the Sacred Marriage
Rite.[10] The *hieros gamos,* which was of great importance in
Mesopotamian religions, entailed a celebration of the consecrated sexual union between the fertility goddess and her consort; it was intended to guarantee the fertility of the land and
to ensure the cyclical order of the seasons (see Kramer 1969).
The prophetic reshaping of this rite had several advantages
from a monotheistic perspective: it required no goddess; it
lent itself to no sexual practices (the nation's sexuality is but
a figure of speech); and it bolstered a cardinal biblical concept:
the covenant.

There are some beautiful and tender prophetic depictions
of the love between God and Israel (particularly in Ezekiel
and Deutero-Isaiah), but the scarcity of such depictions, not
to mention the lack of sexual rites, must have left much to be
desired.[11] The prophets, who offer a profusion of detailed
chastisements concerning Israel's wanton ways, become
rather reticent when dealing with blissful erotic moments
between God and the nation. Worse, even these brief
moments are set in a distant eschatological future. In his
insightful analysis of this phenomenon, Gerson D. Cohen
argues that the Song filled precisely this gap in the prophetic
metaphor. It offered a vocabulary through which the believer
could articulate "in the here and now his affirmation of, and
his delight in, God's love" (1966:13). Thus, regardless of the
original intentions of the writer(s) of the Song, it had the
potential of filling a religious need. This is something Rabbi
Akiva probably had in mind when, on the one hand, he pro-
hibited the singing of these love songs in banquet houses and,
on the other hand, ensured their circulation in a religious context.

The refraction of the intentions of the canon-makers was probably facilitated by the fact that love is never literally consummated in the Song. While the Song's treatment of Eros is unusual in the biblical context, it differs unmistakably from celebrations of erotica in Mesopotamian divine love lyrics. Sumerian texts on the Sacred Marriage, which have often been compared to the Song by what Pope (1977) calls the "cultic interpreters,"[12] are replete with explicit and graphic depictions of the wondrous sexual adventures of the goddess Inanna (whose Semitic name is Ishtar) and her consort Dumuzi (the Tammuz of the Semites). To give but one example:

> The queen bathes her holy loins,
> Inanna bathes for the holy loins of Dumuzi,
> She washes herself with soap.
> She sprinkles sweet-smelling cedar oil on the ground.
>
> The king goes with lifted head to the holy loins,
> Dumuzi goes with lifted head to the holy loins of Inanna.
> He lies down beside her on the bed.
> Tenderly he caresses her, murmuring words of love:
> "O my holy jewel! O my wondrous Inanna!"
>
> After he enters her holy vulva, causing the queen to rejoice,
> After he enters her holy vulva, causing Inanna to rejoice,
> Innana holds him to her and murmers:
> "O Dumuzi, you are truly my love."[13]

Unlike the Sumerian texts, the Song maintains a fascinating tension between chastity and sexual freedom. This is most evident in the representation of the Shulamite. The Shulamite is both a "locked garden" (4:12) and an open one: "Let my beloved come to his garden and enjoy its luscious fruits" (4:16). And she can remain in this paradoxical position, for sexual union in the Song takes place only on a figurative level; and even then it is often anticipated in a jussive verbal tense instead of being narrated in perfect tense.[14] No one literally "enters her vulva."[15]

The ambiguous sexual situation of the Shulamite lends itself to astonishingly different interpretations. She has been hailed both for her chastity and for her uninhibited eroticism. The Shulamite has, on the one hand, been identified with the Blessed Virgin by the Roman Catholic Church, and, on the other hand, portrayed as an agent of free love by modern critics. She is, however, equally removed from both poles.

Desire reigns in the Song, not fulfillment; and in this sense the Song adheres to the biblical worldview. In the Hebrew Bible there is an urgent desire for fulfillment, but by and large—both in the characterization of God, who cannot be incarnated, and in the representations of humankind—fulfillment is denied.[16]

The Song's inclusion in the Bible may be perceived as a case of what Stephen Greenblatt calls "metaphorical acquisition." According to Greenblatt, "metaphorical acquisition works by teasing out latent homologies, similitudes, systems of likeness, but it depends equally upon a deliberate distancing or distortion that precedes the disclosure of likeness" (1988:11). The Song offers a celebration of carnal pleasures reminiscent of Mesopotamian divine love lyrics, teasing out latent homologies which the prophets were reluctant to elaborate. At the same time, it maintains a distance from paganism both by deferring the consummation of sexual desire and by adhering to the human sphere. After all, the Shulamite and her lover are not gods.

Constructions of Gender

Just as the erotic character of the Song was attractive owing to its very otherness, so the rare antipatriarchal bent of this text, I suggest, had something to offer. Despite its socio-ideological alterity, the representation of the relationship between the lovers as an egalitarian one might have been alluring, even to advocates of patriarchy, because of its implications on the allegorical level.

Let me explain. The prophets use the patriarchal marital model in depicting the relationship between God and Israel to highlight, among other things, the hierarchal structure of the covenental bond. This is particularly tangible in Hosea, where the prophet's marital problems with his wife, Gomer, are presented as an exact replica of God's disappointment in the nation. The respective stories of Hosea and God intermingle in a strange way from the very beginning, where the Lord says to the prophet: "Go, take unto thee a wife of whoredoms . . . for the land hath committed great whoredom, departing from the Lord" (1:2). What the conflation of Hosea and God further prescribes is a similar punitive system. God, like a typical patriarchal husband, has the right to inflict much pain on His Bride in response to her disrespectful violation of His Law.

Hence the antipatriarchal model of love in the Song could be made to function as a countervoice to the misogynist prophetic degradation of the nation. It could offer an inspiring consolation in its emphasis on reciprocity. For once the relationship of God and His bride relies on mutual courting, mutual attraction, and mutual admiration, there is more room for hope that redemption is within reach.[17]

The uniqueness and charm of the unusual egalitarian approach of the Song is hinted at in the following midrashic commentary: "In all other hymns [in the Bible] either the Almighty sings the praises of Israel, or Israel sing the praises of the Almighty . . . However, only here in the Song of Songs their hymn to God is answered by a hymn to them. Thus God praises Israel, saying [Song 1:15]: 'Behold thou art fair, my love; behold thou art fair'; and Israel responds with a paean to Him: 'Behold, Thou art fair, my Beloved, yea, pleasant'" (Song of Songs Rabbah 1:11, quoted in Cohen 1966:14). The rabbis do not mention the fact that God rarely praises Israel "in all other hymns," but their emphasis on the unparalleled dialogic character of love in the Song seems to disclose a desire for a break, albeit limited, from the conventional hierarchical representation of the amorous bond between God and the nation.[18]

But the Song is not entirely "depatriarchalized," as Phyllis Trible would have it. Here too one can trace certain marks of mitigation within the text itself which probably facilitated its canonization. The dialogue between the lovers does embrace equality, but it is set within a patriarchal environment, which Trible simply ignores. There are rather hostile male groups—the watchmen and the brothers—who strive to set limits to the Shulamite's unconventional sexual conduct.[19] Sexual regulation, in other words, relies on patriarchal presuppositions: it is primarily intended to control female eroticism. What concerns the watchmen and the brothers, after all, is the Shulamite's virginity, not the chastity of her lover.

Refraction Revisited

My analysis of the needs that the otherness of the Song might have filled by no means implies that the canon-makers were in full control of the evocations of the text. No matter how forceful the yoking of the Song to religious and national purposes might have seemed, the canonization of a secular work in which female eroticism is presented so favorably—a rare phenomenon not only in the Bible, but in Western culture as a whole—remains an astonishing phenomenon.[20] If earlier I stressed the notion that the otherness of the text did not go unnoticed, now I would like to add that the canonization of the Song must have also depended on a certain amount of blindness on the rabbis' part.

In this respect I join those who have challenged Bakhtin's attribution of absolute power to the author's refraction (see Morson and Emerson 1989). In his representation of the coercive light ray, Bakhtin curiously betrays the "dialogical principle" he so ardently endorses elsewhere. If indeed the prose writer compels other voices to yield *fully* to the intentions of the authorial voice, as Bakhtin suggests, then there is no room for exotopy, there is no room for a dialogism which thinks through the radical exteriority of one voice with regard to any other. We may also wonder whether a writer who admits heteroglossia can be in full command of the intentions of other voices, especially alien ones. If this is true of the heteroglot novel, it is all the more relevant when dealing with a text whose compiling depended not on one individual, but presumably on a variety of schools from different periods.

Dreams and Walls

How the Song both challenges the Law and abides by it will, I hope, become apparent through an extended analysis of the tension between the Shulamite and the vigilant male groups, between female eroticism and patriarchal restrictions. But before undertaking such an analysis, let me say a few words about the formal peculiarities of the Song. As Harold Fisch argues, "We do not have anything resembling an Aristotelian unity of action . . . the poem seems to be a jumble of different lyrics and snatches of story . . . we move unexpectedly from the rocky cliffs to the nut garden . . . from the Lebanon in the north to Engedi by the Dead Sea" (1988:89). And then there are sudden shifts in the representation of characters which create a peculiar fluidity. The lover is at times a king and at times a shepherd, a phenomenon that led Ginzburg

(1970), as well as other critics, to construct a far-fetched triangular plot according to which King Solomon courted the Shulamite, but she remained admirably faithful to her rustic lover. The lover, however, is not the only unstable character in the Song. Other figures unexpectedly exchange roles, blend with one another, or simply disappear suddenly. Finally, I should add, the abrupt transitions from literal sites, which turn out to have figurative meanings, to metaphors, which are literalized or elaborated to the extent of turning into conceits, surely contribute to the confusion.[21]

This confusion may be accounted for if, as Fisch suggests, "we recognize in the poem the free flow of images and the shifting kaleidoscope of a dream" (1988:89). There are two passages which are identifiable dreamlike sequences (3:1–5 and 5:2–8), but their mood colors the supposedly waking passages as well. Throughout the entire text there is constant oscillation between the incoherent movement of a dream and concrete reality, between wakefulness and imaginary wakefulness.

I will begin my analysis with one of the identifiable dreamlike sequences, which opens with a dialogue between the lovers and ends with the Shulamite's disturbing account of her encounter with the keepers of the walls.

> I sleep, but my heart waketh: it is the voice of my beloved that knocketh, saying, Open to me, my sister, my love, my dove, my undefiled: for my head is filled with dew, and my locks with the drops of night. I have put off my coat; how shall I put it on? I have washed my feet; how shall I defile them? My beloved put in his hand by the hole of the door, and my bowels were moved for him. I rose up to open to my beloved; and my hands dropped with myrrh, and my fingers with sweet smelling myrrh, upon the handles of the lock. I opened to my beloved; but my beloved had withdrawn himself, and was gone: my soul failed when he spake: I sought him, but I could not find him; I called him, but he gave me no answer. The

watchmen that went about the city found me, they smote me, they wounded me; the keepers of the walls took away my veil from me. I charge you, O daughters of Jerusalem, if ye find my beloved, that ye tell him, that I am sick of love.   (5:2–8)

The beautiful opening verse, "I sleep, but my heart waketh," is both a marker of an oneiric mode of consciousness and a reminder of love's power to rouse. The verb *'ur* (to wake, arouse, rouse) is one of the key words in the Song, most conspicuous in the recurrent adjuration of the Shulamite. Time and again she warns the daughters of Jerusalem not to wake love till it pleases, suggesting that love is too strong a power to arouse without caution. For once this force is set into motion, it does not cease to stir, whether one is awake or asleep.

The sleeping Shulamite, whose heart is wide awake, is beckoned by her lover to rise and open what is usually taken to be the door. Yet the door is never really mentioned, which is why the lover's request calls for double readings. Is the lover, whose locks are filled with "the drops of night," asking his beloved to unlock the door, is he trying to gain access to her body, or both? Here as elsewhere in the Song, supposedly literal verses lend themselves to a figurative reading. Nothing remains purely literal; nothing can escape erotic coloring.

Whether the Shulamite actually rises and speaks to her lover or dreams of doing so, we have here a daring, though curiously indirect, description of sexual arousal. The Shulamite's account of how her lover thrusts his hand through the "hole" is suggestive enough, but so is her response. The King James translation, "and my bowels were moved for him," like the new JPS translation, "and my heart was stirred for him," emphasizes the beloved's emotional response, ignoring the sexual innuendoes of the expression *ume'ay hamu 'alav* in this context. The word *me'ayim* primarily designates the inward parts of the body (the intestines, in particular), which are considered, figuratively speaking, to be the seat of emotions. This term, however, on occasion, stands (in a kind of metonymic assimilation) for the procreative organs. In Genesis 25:23, Isaiah 49:1, and Psalms 71:6 it appears in poetic parallelism with *beten* in the sense of womb (Pope 1977:519–520). Given the exuberent eroticism of this text, the latter meaning of *me'ayim* is surely activated, allowing for a literalization of the expression. The stirring, in other words, takes place on a literal level as well as on a figurative one; it affects the womb at least as much as it affects the soul.

If in the previous sequence the lover likened the beloved to a "spring shut up" *(ma'ayan chatum),* referring particularly, one may assume, to her virginal womb—given the similarity in shape, texture (liquidity), and function (a life-giving substance) of wombs and springs—at this point the dripping of myrrh from the beloved's body suggests that the spring is not entirely sealed, that the beloved's genital juices "flow forth" in quest of an opening. The phonetic similarity of *me'ay* (my inwards or womb) and *ma'ayan* (spring), as well as the aquatic connotations of the verb *hmh*—which is used, among other things, to define the stirring or roar of the sea—reinforce this notion.

The nocturnal encounter "upon the handles of the lock," which comes close to a masturbatory fantasy (the dripping fingers),[22] reaches a climactic point when the beloved yields to her lover's request and finally "opens to him." But just then, on the threshold of sexual climax, her lover vanishes, and she is denied the possibility of consummating her desire. The tension between desire and fulfillment remains.

Now the lovers reverse roles: the Shulamite sets out to seek her loved one. Wandering about the city streets, she encounters the keepers of the walls, who beat her and strip off her veil. The fact that these are male guards who harass only the Shulamite underscores the patriarchal character of the society within which the amorous dialogue takes place.

Sexual freedom and its spatial correlate (free wandering) is a male prerogative. A woman who acts upon her desire runs the risk of being abused and shamed. This does not mean that the Song is uncritical of the guardians of the Law. Since the Shulamite is the focalizer, we cannot help but identify with her yearnings to find her loved one, with her struggle to break loose. A comparison between this nocturnal pursuit and similar episodes in Hosea and Ezekiel, where the Guards are the focalizers, may highlight the Song's unusual treatment of female eroticism.[23]

In the opening chapters of Hosea the prophet (assuming God's role) chastises his wife (Israel) for chasing after her lovers. Recounting her sins to her children, he says:

Plead with your mother, plead: for she is not my wife, neither am I her husband: let her therefore put away her whoredoms out of her sight, and her adulteries from between her breasts; Lest I strip her naked, and set her as in the day that she was born, and make her as a wilderness, and set her like a dry land, and slay her with thirst. And I will not have mercy upon her children; for they be the children of whoredoms. For their mother hath played the harlot: she that conceived them hath done shamefully: for she said, I will go after my lovers, that give me my bread and my water, my wool and my flax, mine oil and my drink. Therefore, behold, I will hedge up thy way with thorns, and make a wall, that she shall not find her paths. And she shall follow after her lovers, but she shall not overtake them; and she shall seek them, but shall not find them: then shall she say, I will go and return to my first husband; for then was it better with me than now. For she did not know that I gave her corn, and wine, and oil, and multiplied her silver and gold, which they prepared for Baal. Therefore will I return, and take away my corn in the time thereof . . . and will recover my wool and my flax given to cover her nakedness. And now will I discover her lewdness in the sight of her lovers, and none shall deliver her out of mine hand. (2:2–10)

Similarly, Ezekiel in the Name of the Lord rebukes Israel for her lewd ways:

> Thus saith the Lord God; Because thy filthiness was poured out, and thy nakedness discovered through thy whoredoms with thy lovers, and with all the idols of thy abominations, and by the blood of thy children, which thou didst give unto them; Behold, therefore I will gather all thy lovers, with whom thou hast taken pleasure, and all them that thou hast loved, with all them that thou hast hated; I will even gather them round about against thee, and will discover thy nakedness unto them, that they may see all thy nakedness.   (16:36–37)

In both prophetic texts female eroticism is synonymous with abomination, promiscuity, and infidelity. Ezekiel depicts the vaginal fluids (translated by King James as "filthiness") that pour out of the female body with disgust. Hosea's misogyny is most poignant in his representation of whoredoms as part and parcel of the female body. "Adulteries" (Hos. 2:2), rather than a "bundle of myrrh" (SoS. 1:13), lie between the woman's breasts.

The two prophets prescribe harsh symmetrical punishments for the wanton. She who eagerly exposed her body to her lovers is doomed to be exposed in public. What she once did for pleasure will now be done to her for her disgrace (see Anderson and Freedman 1980:249). To further understand the sin and punishment, one needs to bear in mind that "uncovering the nakedness" is a biblical expression designating illicit sexual relations (from incest to adultery). Conversely, "covering the nakedness," as is evident in both Hosea 2:11 and Ezekiel 16:8, is a synonym for marriage. This opposition in terms, as Rachel Biale suggests (1984:178–179), reveals the two poles in the biblical notion of sexual mores: legitimate conjugal sexual relations are kept "under covers," while illicit sexual ties are regarded as a shameful exposure.

Interestingly, such (un)covering has implications in the realm of representation. What remains "under covers" is in a sense unrepresentable, whereas illicit sexuality must be exposed as a mode of punishment. This is one way of explaining why the Prophets indulge in detailed descriptions of Israel's promiscuity, but say very little about her sexual desire at eschatological moments when she regrets her sins and reunites with her Bridegroom.

The prophetic preoccupation with female nakedness (Ephraim, the male personification of the nation is never uncovered) seems to exhibit an all too common patriarchal need to control women's bodies and women's sexuality (see Suleiman 1985), to make clear distinctions between women whose bodies are owned by given men (father, brother, or husband) and those who may be regarded as public property. There are no biblical laws on women's attire, but the prophetic punishments call to mind the Assyrian legislation regarding (un)veiling, which Gerda Lerner calls attention to in *The Creation of Patriarchy*. According to Assyrian law, "Neither [wives] of [seigniors] nor [widows] . . . who go out on the street may have their heads uncovered. The daughters of a seignior . . . whether it is a shawl or a robe or [a mantle], must veil themselves . . . when they go out on the street alone, they must veil themselves. A concubine who goes out on the street with her mistress must veil herself . . . A harlot must not veil herself; her head must be uncovered" (1986:134). This is why, Lerner explains, "unauthorized veiling" is regarded as a great offense, so much so that castigation consists of public whipping and stripping naked in the street.

The punishment that Ezekiel and Hosea mete out in the name of the Ultimate Keeper and the Assyrian law shed light on the watchmen's behavior in the Song. Their stripping off of the Shulamite's veil reveals the same symmetrical logic. A woman who does not maintain her nakedness under cover exposes herself to the danger of being undressed in public.

There are, however, significant differences between the Song and the Prophets. In Hosea and Ezekiel the severe response of God is represented as the expression of Ultimate Justice. His stripping of the nation seems almost moderate, given her ingratitude. One is expected to take pity on God for having to play such a violent role, for having to suffer so for the sake of Law and Order. This is particularly poignant in Hosea, whose poetics have been defined by Harold Fisch (1985:136–157) as a "poetics of violence." Conversely, in the Song, where we are taken into the scene through the Shulamite's eyes, the watchmen seem reactionary, merciless, and excessively aggressive.

But there is more. The Song disrupts the polar structure of the biblical notion of sexual mores and the concomitant conventions of representation. The Shulamite is neither covered nor uncovered. We do not know to what extent she actually exposes her body to her lover or to anyone else for that matter. The keepers of the wall may treat her as a wanton, but her conduct is different. "I have put off my coat; how shall I put it on?" she asks her lover, but teasingly remains naked behind the door. How well the Shulamite is dressed when she finally "opens up" and roams about in the streets is left to speculation. And there is always the possibility that she never actually exposes herself to public humiliation; her roaming about in the streets, like her encounter with the watchmen, may be yet another episode in a dream. What I am suggesting is that the blurring of boundaries between dream and reality in the Song, like the nebulous demarcation between figurative and literal levels, plays a role in maintaining the beloved's indeterminate status between covered nakedness and uncovered nakedness.

Perhaps (if she actually does wander around incompletely dressed) we have here a specimen of one of the typical dreams Freud describes in *The Interpretation of Dreams,* "dreams of being naked or insufficiently dressed in the presence of strangers" (1957:242). In other words, the Shulamite's nocturnal outing may be perceived as an oneiric expression of what Freud calls the "desire to exhibit." Later, she explicitly expresses a similar wish when yearning to kiss her lover in public without being put to shame: "O that thou wert as my brother, that sucked the breasts of my mother! when I should find thee without, I would kiss thee; yea, I should not be despised" (8:1). It is a wish to return to a paradisiacal phase—infancy—in which nakedness and desire (even an incestuous one, "O that thou wert as my *brother*") can be exhibited without shame (see Freud 1957: 245).

But as is often the case in dreams of exhibiting, here too forbidden wishes fall victim to repression. Watchmen, after all, are a most appropriate personification of inhibitory forces. Freud himself uses this metaphor when describing the dynamics of censorship. He likens the system of the unconscious "to a large entrance hall, in which the mental impulses jostle one another like separate individuals. Adjoining this entrance hall there is a second, narrower, room—a kind of drawing-room—in which consciousness, too, resides. But on the threshold between these two rooms a watchman performs his function: he examines the different mental impulses, acts as a censor, and will not admit them into the drawing-room if they displease him" (1957:295).

The harshness with which the watchmen in the Song attempt to control the jostling impulses at the "threshold" turns this episode into a distressing anxiety-dream, a nightmare of sorts (see Pope 1977:134). Trible, who treats the Song as if it were a representation of a harmonic "garden" of wish-fulfillment where the lovers enjoy sex and wander about naked "without shame or fear" (1978:161), fails to see not only the lack of fulfillment in the text but also its nonidyllic presentation of love, the anxiety and shame that accompany the pleasures of exposure, especially when a female body is at stake.

The lover's elaborate descriptions of the Shulamite's body (the so-called *wasfs*) provide no conclusive answer with respect to her exposure. They hover between representations of a naked body and a covered one. Even at points where the Shulamite's breasts and navel (or perhaps vagina; see 7:2) are depicted, one cannot tell whether or not it is the lover's imagination which is at work. The intricate metaphorical play whereby each one of the beloved's body parts is likened to another object (for example, "Thy two breasts are like two young roes that are twins, which feed among the lilies" 4:5), may in fact create an impression that the lover is attempting to fill in the gaps in his knowledge of her body, using as many vehicles as he can to grasp the tenor.

To return to the Shulamite's nocturnal encounter by the walls, one may well ask to what extent the guards are successful in blocking her way. They may have disrupted her pursuit, but they haven't really stopped her. In the following sequence (although it is impossible to speak of a coherent plot in the Song, the order of sequences, as in dreams, is not without significance) the Shulamite, breathless as usual, recruits the daughters of Jerusalem to help her find her lover. The search goes on.

That the watchmen's control is not absolute is made clear in the first dreamlike sequence (3:1–4). Here too the Shulamite is driven by her desire to wander about the streets at night in search of her loved one. Upon being found by the watchmen, she desperately asks: "Saw ye him whom my soul loveth?" No reply is given. The Shulamite moves on. Perhaps the beloved cannot bear to wait for an answer, anxious as she is to find her lover. Perhaps she realizes that the watchmen are about to harass her and decides to avoid the danger. However one interprets this abrupt transition, the Shulamite does manage to pass by the guards and find her lover.

What is at stake then is a dialectic between wishes and restrictions. Whenever desire seems to be beyond control, it is in one way or another restrained; and vice versa, whenever the censors seem to prevail, they end up being circumvented.

The Changing of the Guard

So far I have focused on the opposition between the Shulamite and the male guards, between female desire and patriarchal constraints. The interrelations between the two forces, however, are far more complex. The Shulamite and the guards have more in common than one may suspect at first. To begin with, both "go about" *(svv)* the streets at night. The guardians of the law, who set out to restrict sexual desires, seem to be motivated by the sort of wishes which haunt their victim. It is worthwhile, as Jane Gallop (following Irigaray) reminds us, "to question the law's appearance of indifference . . . to lift the mantle of the law" (1982:77), which seeks to protect its male guardians from female eroticism, and to expose the desire of the legislators. By stripping off the Shulamite's veil, the watchmen intend to punish her for her wanton ways; but at the same time their punitive methods seem to lay bare their own desire to uncover. Much like the sixty (!) heroes who guard King Solomon's bed "because of fear in the night" *(mipachad baleylot),* each with his "sword" on the "thigh" (3:8), so the keepers of the walls are probably acting on their desires in their very attempt to control "the night."

Similarly, the Shulamite's eroticism is restrained not only by male guards but also through her own guarding. She hesitates to open to her lover long before she meets the guards. To be sure, internalized patriarchal restrictions seem to be at work in the latter case, but there is more. Sick as she is with love, overwhelmed by its immense power, the Shulamite may be seeking walls as a means of maintaining her equilibrium. She too seems fearful of the night.

Little wonder then that the Shulamite herself is portrayed as a guard at various points in the Song: "My mother's children were angry with me; they made me the keeper of the vineyards; but mine own vineyard have I not kept" (1:6). Not unlike the watchmen, she is far from being a perfect guard. She has not been too successful in keeping her vineyard (the vineyard seems to serve as yet another metaphor for the Shulamite's body) from intruders. But one cannot tell whether she is bragging about her unguarded vineyard or worried about it. What does seem to be clear is that the Shulamite's conduct upsets those who *made* her the keeper of the vineyards, namely, her brothers.

The conflict between the Shulamite and her brothers with respect to vigilance and virginity resurges in a fascinating exchange at the very end of the Song: "We have a little sister, and she hath no breasts: what shall we do for our sister in the day when she shall be spoken for? If she be a wall, we will build upon her a palace of silver: and if she be a door, we will inclose her with boards of cedar. I am a wall, and my breasts like towers: then was I in his eyes as one that found favour" (8:8–10).

The intricate transitions from semiliteral settings to metaphorical ones in the Song is quite remarkable. Both the wall and the door (opening), which were partially concrete in chapter 5, become at this point explicit vehicles whose tenor is the beloved's body. The brothers, once again concerned with their sister's chastity, liken her to a wall and a door which must be fortified and guarded in the face of coming dangers, that is, in the face of her coming sexual ripeness. The similarity (merging almost) between the brothers and the watchmen is now made clear: both male groups watch over walls in a rather hostile manner! I assume that in the brothers' case as well forbidden desires have something to do with the insistence upon blocking the Shulamite's body. Their scheme to lock her up when she comes of age seems to reveal—in addition to a concern with her value as a means of circulation—an incestuous desire to defer the moment in which they will have to hand over their beloved sister to another guard—her spouse. Is that why they overlook the fact that their "little sister" already has breasts?

At this point, more openly than before, the Shulamite teases those who attempt to set limits to her desires (see Falk 1982:132). She turns her brothers' simile into a metaphor: "I am a wall," she proclaims, as if to reinforce the validity of their statement. But then she provocatively refutes their capacity to guard her. Blind as they are to her sexual maturation, to her "towering" breasts, their ability to shield her virginity is called into question.

The beloved's likening of her breasts to towers also indicates her feminine strength. In what seems a parody of Freud's depiction of penis envy, of the "disappointing moment" when the little girl discovers that unlike her brother she has no penis, the beloved makes clear that, despite her siblings' statement, she lacks nothing. Quite the contrary. She has two breasts as mighty and powerful as two towers; she is strong enough to watch over her body without the vigilance of her inept brothers.

The Shulamite's boastful depiction of her fortification however, does not necessarily affirm that the purpose of her strength is to chase away potential invaders. Perhaps she further teases her brothers by suggesting that military structures may be useful in making love and not war. With the help of her "towers," she has after all allured her loved one; she has—and the following translation is a literal one—"found peace [*motset shalom*] in his eyes" (8:10). Marcia Falk's rendition of this obscure verse is to my mind the most convincing one: "So I have found peace / Here with my lover." (The King James Version ignores the "peaceful" element in this response.) The Shulamite's formidable fortification, in other words, brings about a peaceful amorous encounter. That the lover is impressed by her might is apparent in his similar metaphorical use of military architecture to depict her body. To give but one example: "Thy neck is like the tower of David builded for an armoury, whereon there hang a thousand bucklers, all shields of mighty men" (4:4).[24]

In her response the Shulamite thus challenges her brothers' perception of virginity.[25] She rejects their possessiveness, their treating her as an object whose value depends on blankness, on having "known no man." She turns her nubility into a mark of subjecthood, power, independence, and self-containment. Like the goddess Inanna who, upon her maturation, sets out to attain a throne and a bed,[26] so the Shulamite is eager to celebrate her ripeness, to take pleasure in her budding powers. "Come, my beloved, let us go forth into the field; let us lodge in the villages. Let us get up early to the vineyards; let us see if the vine flourish, whether the tender grape appear, and the pomegranates bud forth: there will I give thee my loves" (7:11–12).

The blossoming plants, she seems to assure her lover, echo her own ripeness and readiness to enjoy womanhood, to indulge in the pleasures of love. But even this rather explicit offer is set in the future. The Shulamite may seek to transcend the city walls at night and sleep in the fields with her loved one, but fulfillment is deferred. Here as elsewhere, she both abides by the Law and challenges it, guards her virginity and opens the door to her lover.

The Keepers of the Torah

According to the midrashic interpretation, the keepers of the wall are "the keepers of the walls of the Torah" (Shir HaShirim Rabbah v. 7). Using this allegorical reading as a springboard, let us return to the opening question. Why was the Song canonized? Let me suggest that the canonmakers, those who set limits to the sacred corpus, were in fact not unlike the keepers of the walls in the Song. Just as the guards in the Song are neither omnipotent nor innocent of forbidden desires, so the watchmen of Holy Writ could not fully prevent the admission of ideologically alien voices within the canon, especially those other voices which filled (unconscious) needs in the biblical array. And the Song too played a role in the drama. If this deviant text could have circumvented the keepers of the walls, it is probably because the Song is not entirely antagonistic to the Law. Like the Shulamite, the Song simultaneously challenges the Law and accepts it, reveals and conceals its otherness.

❧ 8 ❧

Conclusion

Throughout my wanderings among various strata of the biblical text I have tried to make the most of broken pieces, scattered histories, condensed naming-speeches, obscure traces of premonotheistic pasts, remnants of dreams, fragments of forgotten pursuits. I have suggested that by paying attention to such bits and pieces, we can reconstruct, if only partially, a fascinating array of counter female voices, without falling into the trap of idealizing the past or endorsing highly speculative and problematic myths, such as the myth of matriarchy.

   I have by no means uncovered all the countertraditions to be found under the thick layers of patriarchal discourses in the Bible. My objective was to present a few exemplary cases to illustrate the diversity of antithetical texts and voices which call into question the predominantly patriarchal base of monotheism. While all the countertraditions I have analyzed share a certain antipatriarchal bent, their mode of revisionism and the topic of their critique differ significantly. What a distance there is between the provocative counterversion of creation offered by Eve and the idyllic revisionism of the Book of Ruth, between Rachel's dream of grandeur and the Shulamite's erotic fantasies, between Zipporah's magical strange words and Miriam's criticism of Moses' privileged status.

In exploring the heterogeneity of biblical representations of femininity, I relied on Bakhtin's observations concerning heteroglot texts. I have suggested that the canon-makers, much like Bakhtin's novelist, sought to create a dialogic interplay between a variety of competing languages and ideologies of different groups from different periods. Bakhtin's model, however, has some drawbacks which I have tackled by setting it against a psychoanalytic model. Thus I questioned the extent to which an author of a heteroglot text, let alone a group of authors, can be fully aware of, or have full control over, the implications of the dialogues he or she creates. I have, in other words, tried to take into account both conscious motives and unconscious longings in my analyses of the ways in which countertraditions have found their way into the Hebrew canon. Needless to say, the demarcation between intentional and unintentional choices is never a clear one, all the more so when dealing with a text whose history is so obscure. Nevertheless, it is necessary, I believe, to make such an interdisciplinary move to understand better the heterogeneity of the Bible. Relying solely on Bakhtin would have meant ignoring some of the striking peculiarities of these countertraditions, the curious marks of censorship. Conversely, to draw solely on Freud would have been to reduce the powerful dialogic imagination which produced this text.

Job's Wife

Let me give one final example: Job's wife.[1] Much has been written by modern readers about the unusual challenge the Book of Job offers in its audacious questioning of the ways of God. One cannot but be amazed by the fact that a text in which God is represented as a torturous unjust deity, with little compassion for human misery (even if this notion is somewhat mitigated at the end), has managed to acquire canonical status. Most of the readings which marvel at the antithetical thrust of the Book of Job focus on the figure of Job, portraying him as a raging rebel who ridicules dogmatic notions of faith in his desperate accusations against God. One never hears of the contribution of Job's wife to the antidogmatic bent of this text. To be sure, she is only a one-line character and as such receives but brief exposure, and yet this one line can reveal a great deal.

But before exploring the startling words of Job's wife, I should comment on the structure of the Book of Job. A conspicuous fissure, which has troubled many readers, separates the prose frame-story from the poetic dialogues. The prose prologue begins with a seemingly naive tale about the "righteous" Job, a God-fearing man of "perfect integrity," who had the best of all worlds: seven sons, three daughters, seven thousand sheep, three thousand camels, five hundred yoke of oxen, five hundred donkeys, and many slaves. One day, in a celestial drama unbeknown to Job, the Adversary (a precursor of the Devil) spurs God to test the disinterestedness of Job's piety by afflicting him. In a succession of tragic events, Job loses his property, his slaves, and then all his children; and yet, in contradistinction to the Adversary's prediction, he does not curse God for inflicting him with such pain. On the contrary, he blesses Him with incredible resignation: "Naked came I out of my mother's womb, and naked shall I return thither: the Lord gave, and the Lord hath taken away; blessed be the name of the Lord" (1:21). And even when Job's own skin becomes the target of the Adversary's tormenting hand, in the second round of calamities, he doesn't succumb to blasphemy.

The transition to the poetic dialogues is quite shocking,

not only because of the poignant generic differences, but also because Job of the dialogues is anything but patient. In a series of exchanges with his friends he insists on his innocence and ardently protests against divine injustice, shaking his fist at God for misconducting His creation, putting Him on trial for bringing unbearable suffering with no reason. This is indeed the impatient Job modern readers have identified with and admired—so much so that the frame-story has been often disregarded as a simplistic supplement of little value.

The discrepancies between the prose frame-story and the poetic bulk of the Book of Job are yet another example of the diversity of languages which intersect in the Hebrew Bible. But here as elsewhere heterogeneity does not preclude inter-textual interactions. The prologue (far more intricate than is often assumed) and the dialogues are not as detached as it may seem at first.

Let me suggest that Job's wife, who appears at the end of the prologue, prefigures or perhaps even generates the impatience of of the dialogues. She turns up after the final blow, after Job has been struck with boils. Seeing her husband sitting in the dust, scraping his sores silently, she bursts out with: "Dost thou still retain thine integrity? curse God, and die" (2:9). She simply cannot bear her husband's blind acceptance of the tragedies which relentlessly befall them, one after the other. She too, after all, is a victim of these divine tests. This is something the Septuagint makes clear as it expands upon the terse original version.

After a long time had passed his wife said to him: "How long will you endure and say, 'See, I will wait a bit longer, looking for the hope of my salvation.' Look, your memory is already blotted out from the earth, (along with) the sons and daughters, the travail and pangs of my womb, whom I reared in toil for nothing. And you, you sit in wormy decay, passing the nights in the open, while I roam and drudge from place to place, and from house to house, waiting for the sun to go down, so that I may rest from my toils and the griefs which now grip me."

To cling to a model of "perfect" devotion to a supposedly "perfect" God when reality is so far from perfection seems to Job's wife not exemplary strength but an act of cowardice. Such "integrity," she seems to be saying, lacks a deeper value. What Job must do is to challenge the God who has afflicted him so, even if the consequence be death.

Job's wife thus opens the possibility of suspending belief, of speaking up against God. Interestingly, Job has been obsessed with the question of speaking against God long before the calamities take place. Whenever his sons and daughters feast together, he offers "burnt offerings according to the number of them all: for Job said, It may be that my sons have sinned, and cursed God in their hearts" (1:5). Job is pious to an extreme: he even fears what his children may unwittingly say in their *hearts!* He seems to be seeking full control over thoughts, let alone speech, but is haunted by the possibility that such control is impossible, especially when other lips and hearts are involved.

When his wife unhesitatingly suggests that God be cursed, she makes it clear that Job indeed has no control over the speech of others. The idea that time and again terrifies Job as he obsessively prepares offerings—that one of his family members would curse God or consider doing so—now has become a disturbing reality. But just as his sacrifices on behalf of his children may disclose an even greater fear that he himself is susceptible to sinning, so his angry response to his wife seems to indicate that he is losing his temper precisely because his wife dares to say something which is on the verge of bursting through his own mouth. "But he said unto her, Thou speakest as one of the foolish women speaketh. What? shall we receive good at the hand of God, and shall we not receive evil?" (2:10) As Moshe Greenberg points out, "the question is rhetorical, but in every rhetorical question lurks the possible affirmation of what is ostensibly denied" (1987:285).

The exchange between Job and his wife concludes with the assertion that "in all this did not Job sin with his lips." The focus on Job's lips is curious and may intimate a certain discrepancy between Job's lips and his "heart."[2]

Despite the fact that the prologue is primarily a story about patience at all costs, it is thus not innocent of moments of impatience. Job's wife initiates a challenge to God, and Job, one could argue, is already on his way to losing his patience. I do not mean to underestimate the friction between the frame-story and the dialogues, rather to suggest that a certain tension between patience and impatience, between blessing and cursing God, is already evident in the prologue. The recurrent use of the word *brkh,* both in the sense of "bless" and, paradoxically, as a euphemism for "curse," throughout the prologue seems to augment the tension between these two antithetical speech acts.

Whatever the original character of these traditions may have been, their combination creates an intriguing psychological drama of transformation.[3] It seems as if the pious Job must undergo various painful phases of awakening before he can call into question the system of beliefs he has cherished for so long. The fissure between the prologue and the dialogues marks the acuteness of the crisis.

When the dialogues begin Job is finally ready to "open his mouth" and curse. Euphemisms are left behind, and the explicit terms for "curse" (*kll* and later *'arr*) appear. Job's anger at his fate now breaks loose:

> After this opened Job his mouth, and cursed his day. And Job spake, and said, Let the day perish wherein I was born, and the night in which it was said, There is a man child con-

ceived . . . Let them curse it that curse the day . . . Let the
stars of the twilight thereof be dark; let it look for light, but
have none; neither let it see the dawning of the day: Because it
shut not up the doors of my mother's womb, not hid sorrow
from mine eyes. Why died I not from the womb? why did I
not give up the ghost when I came out of the belly? Why did
the knees prevent me? or why the breasts that I should
suck?   (3:1–12)

Job, who rebuked his wife for speaking like a "foolish"
woman, now comes close to doing what she had suggested.
He does not curse God directly, but by cursing his birth he
implicitly curses the Creator who gave him life. At this point
Job is willing to "curse and die." Living in a world run by a
merciless God is unbearable for him. The best he can wish
for is not to have been conceived at all, or at least not to have
been born.

What is more, Job of the dialogues seems to be treating
his friends just as his wife treated him—as dogmatic believers
who overlook the discrepancies between their system of
beliefs and the bleak reality. He does not hesitate to suggest
that God "destroyeth the perfect and the wicked. If the
scourge slay suddenly, he will laugh at the trial of the innocent. The earth is given into the hand of the wicked: he cov-
ereth the faces of the judges thereof; if not, where, and who
is he?" (9:22–24).

In the face of his friends' insistence that God adheres to
the doctrine of retribution, he argues that to believe in such a
doctrine means to be blind to what actually takes place in the
world, for calamities may fall indiscriminately both on the
righteous and the wicked. Worse, to God's rather sadistic
delight, the wicked, far more than the "perfect," thrive and
prosper.

Job's wife has been defined by Augustine as "the helpmeet of the devil" *(adiutrix diaboli)* for enticing her husband

to challenge God. Augustine was right to suggest that Job's wife brings Job closer to fulfilling the Adversary's prediction ("he will curse thee to thy face"), but he fails to see that the Book of Job ends up endorsing a rather "impatient" form of faith. Even God, in the prose epilogue, makes clear that he prefers Job's protest against divine injustice to the dogmatic, thoughtless faith of the friends. Much like Eve, the well-known "helpmeet" to whom Augustine alludes, Job's wife spurs her husband to doubt God's use of His powers, but in doing so she does him much good, for this turns out to be the royal road to deepen one's knowledge, to open one's eyes. Through his questioning of divine conduct, Job realizes that the world defies comfortable moral categorizings and that God (like most biblical characters for that matter) does not yield to fixed epithets such as "just" and "perfect."⁴ And once Job is capable of releasing himself, as Kahn puts it, from "insistence on exact measure" (p. 153) in his relationship with God, he discovers a far more intricate mode of faith, a faith which relies on an ongoing quest. Or as Bakhtin defines it in a brief reference to the Book of Job: "In its structure Job's dialogue is internally endless, for the opposition of the soul to God—whether the opposition be hostile or humble— is conceived in it as something irrevocable and eternal" (1984:280).

Beyond Piety

The transformation Job undergoes in his perception of God is accompanied by a change in his approach to human relations. Job, at first, is something of a workaholic, so immersed in his worship of God that there seems to be no room in his life for mere human beings. He summons his children to purify themselves before God, under his auspices, after each banquet that they throw, but he never participates in their feasts. Similarly, his first response to the calamities is "to go back to work," to bless God, and to seclude himself from society. He sits apart on the ground when his wife approaches him. Her cry may be interpreted not only as a challenge to divine conduct, but also as a criticism of her husband's very obsession with God, an obsession which draws him away from his family and allows him to repress all that disrupts his pious routine: the death of his children, the fall of his household—and the agony of his wife.

The exchange between Job and his wife and later between Job and his friends—regardless of how hostile these dialogues tend to be—mark the beginning of Job's growing interest in human relations. This tendency reaches its peak in the epilogue. At this point Job reconciles with the friends with whom he had argued so vehemently. What is more, he becomes a host. "Then came there unto him all his brethren, and all his sisters, and all they that had been of his acquaintance before, and did eat bread with him in his house: and they bemoaned him, and comforted him over all the evil that the Lord had brought upon him: every man also gave him a piece of money, and every one an earring of gold" (42:11). Job finally is having a gathering in his own house—and quite a gathering—all of his siblings and all those whom he had known in the good old days show up. He is no longer worried about what his kin may think in their hearts, nor does he feel rejected (something he complains about at length throughout the dialogues).[5] He welcomes his visitors, *eats* with them (Job never ate with anyone before in this text), accepts their condolences and even some worldly goods. Job finally realizes that piety is not everything. The Book of Job thus makes clear that an intense dialogue with God does not preclude other dialogues. On the contrary, it enhances an openness to other modes of intimacy and is, in turn, enriched by them.

Fragrant Names

Even more fascinating, Job's relation to women undergoes a significant change. The man who rebuked and silenced his wife and later, in the dialogues, expressed continual anger at the female body that gave birth to him, now behaves differently. The difference is apparent in Job's exceptional treatment of his three daughters. To begin with, he names them (curiously their brothers remain unnamed). This is actually the only place in the Bible where a father names his daughters! In Chapter 3 I suggested that in contrast to what is usually assumed, female characters in the Bible often give names but rarely have the privilege of having their own naming recounted. To record the act of naming means, among other things, to accentuate the importance of a given birth, of a given child, which is why such attention is—with few exceptions—[6] denied to daughters in the Bible. Job, however, undermines these patriarchal conventions and endows his daughters with captivating names which match their renowned beauty: Bright Day (or possibly Dove), Cassia (a type of perfume), and Horn of Antimony (a black powder used to beautify the eyes). These exotic names have nothing to do with piety. They speak of a new world Job has discovered, a world of beauty, of fragrance, of cosmetics—of feminine grace.[7]

Job expresses his respect for his daughters not only by naming them but also by providing them with property. Job, we are told, gave his daughters "inheritance among their brethren" (42:15). According to biblical law, only in the absence of male heirs were daughters permitted to receive their father's estate.[8] Here, therefore, is a clear deviation from the law, for Job's daughters inherit, despite the fact that they have brothers. As Stephen Mitchell beautifully puts it: "There is something enormously satisfying about this prominence of

the feminine at the end of *Job* . . . It is as if, once Job has
learned to surrender, his world too gives up the male com-
pulsion to control. The daughters have almost the last word.
They appear with the luminous power of figures in a dream:
we can't quite figure out why they are so important, but we
know that they are" (1987: xxx).

Coming across these female names is like finding among
the debris of a ruined ancient site three perfume bottles which
have miraculously remained intact, bearing, even though
empty, the aroma of a lost tradition.

But where is Job's nameless wife? She is conspicuously
absent from the happy ending in which Job's world is
restored. One may well ask why. While Job's dead children
spring back to life, as it were, for he now has, just as in the
beginning, seven sons and three daughters, his wife, who
actually managed to escape death, is curiously excluded from
this scene of familial bliss. Let me suggest that here too censorship is at work. It is no accident that Job's wife does not
benefit from her husband's changed relation to femininity in
the epilogue. Although in a sense her words give rise to Job's
criticism of the ways of God, they remain far too antithetical
to allow her reappearance. The challenge of the outsider—
and woman is something of an outsider in divine-human
affairs—seems far more threatening than a critique voiced
from within.

In my analysis of the Book of Job I have focused on secondary figures in the prologue and epilogue who hitherto
have received scant scholarly attention. Despite their margin-
ality, however, Job's wife and daughters have the power to
shed a different light on the Book of Job. By exploring their
roles, I have tried to tease out of this text an antithetical bent,
however limited, to patriarchal conventions. I have also tried
to show that here as elsewhere various oppositional voices
coexist, for the unconventional approach to God interestingly
intermingles with an unconventional approach to femininity.

Open House

If I have evoked Job's wife to conclude, it is not only because
she is another fine example of what we can do with frag-
mented histories but also because her challenge is compatible
with a certain line of inquiry in feminist criticism which I
wholly endorse. Feminist criticism is at its best, I think,
when, like Job's wife, it avoids taking truths for granted,
when it lays bare the problematic presuppositions of given
belief systems. And such inquiries are essential not only with
regard to patriarchal theories, but also as an internal critique,
that is, with respect to feminist theories and assumptions. For
some, the latter critical move seems to endanger the strength
and impact of feminist criticism.[9] I believe, on the contrary,
that the very growth of the field depends on a continual questioning of its base, on a continual quest for a better understanding of gender constructions and the ways in which such
constructions may change in the course of time.

I have tried to show throughout this book that if such a
line of inquiry is taken in reading the Bible, if we avoid
patriarchalizing or depatriarchalizing it and defy comfortable
categorizings of the biblical stance on gender issues, then
unknown reaches of the past may open out before us, revealing faded figures of female precursors who, through their
very otherness, have the striking capacity to add much color
and intensity to our own lives.

That the past—if we open ourselves up to it—may add
unexpected pleasures to present pursuits is something that the
Shulamite already seems to be aware of. In a beautiful passage
in the Song of Songs, she draws her lover's attention to the
apple tree under which she aroused his love and reminds him
that this is the very tree under which his mother conceived
and then bore him: "I raised thee up under the apple tree:
there thy mother [conceived] thee: there she brought thee
forth that bare thee" (8:5). She seems to seek a sense of con-

tinuity with the past. As if the past had the power to add an attractive layer to the present, as if the present were inconceivable without reinscribing the mother's history into it. In this case it is the lover's mother, but the Shulamite's own mother holds a similar attraction, for at times the Shulamite's greatest yearning—surprising as it may first seem—is to take her lover not to the fields, but rather to her mother's house: "I held him, and would not let him go, until I had brought him into my mother's house, and into the chamber of her that conceived me" (3:4).

The mother's house is a rare construction. It appears only in the story of Rebekah, in the Book of Ruth, and in the Song of Songs.[10] Elsewhere the father's house prevails. The rarity of the mother's house, however, need not diminish our desire to seek it. If the Shulamite insists with such urgency that her loved one come with her, it is precisely because exploring the mother's house has so much to offer to all.

Notes
Bibliography
Index

Notes

1. Preliminary Excavations

1. For more on Freud's use of the archaeological metaphor, see Kuspit (1989).

2. "Higher Criticism" was set against the so-called "Lower Criticism." The latter attempted to establish the original text of Scripture free from mistranslations.

3. In the third chapter of *A Room of One's Own,* Virginia Woolf (after searching in vain in historical books for an extensive depiction of women in the Elizabethan period) reconstructs the imaginary fate of Judith Shakespeare (whose apocryphal name is of course not accidental), a woman in the Elizabethan period who was as wonderfully gifted as Shakespeare was. The history of "Shakespeare's sister" is by now well known. Unlike her brother, who received a fairly extensive education, who studied Latin and the elements of grammar and logic, who poached rabbits outdoors, and later conquered the stage, Judith was not sent to school and managed only rarely to scribble some pages (in between domestic chores). As adventurous and imaginative as her brother, Judith decides one day to run away from home and try her luck in the London theater. "She stood at the stage door; she wanted to act, she said. Men laughed in her face. The manager . . . bellowed something about poodles dancing and women acting—no woman, he said, could possibly be an actress . . . Yet her genius was for fiction and lusted to feed abundantly upon the lives of men and women and the study of their ways . . . at last Nick Greene the actor-manager took pity on her; she found herself with child by that gentleman and so— who shall measure the heat and violence of the poet's heart when caught

and tangled in a woman's body?—killed herself one winter's night and lies buried at some cross-roads where the omnibuses now stop outside the Elephant and Castle" (1929:49–50).

4. For a similar observation, see Trible (1989). For more on Miriam, see Plaskow (1990).

5. Here and in later citations from the Bible, I use the King James Version, unless otherwise indicated.

6. One notable exception is the remarkable poem "Miriam" of the modern Hebrew woman poet Yocheved Bat-Miriam. I should add that in running commentaries, that is, commentaries such as the Midrash, which expound each and every verse of Scripture, we do find interpretations of this passage.

7. The Midrash tries to fill in some of the gaps. In addition to providing Miriam with prophecies that justify her title, it attributes to her a miraculous well. The well appears in an interpretation of Micah 6:4. According to the rabbis, the merit of the three deliverers ensured that the children of Israel would receive various divine gifts: Moses' merit was rewarded by manna; because of Aaron's merit clouds of glory shielded the wanderers, and "the well was due to the merit of Miriam, who sang by the waters of the Red sea; as it is said: *And Miriam sang (wa-ta'an) unto them: Sing ye to the Lord* (Ex. xv, 21), and by the waters of the well, *Then sang Israel this song, Rise up, O well, sing ('enu) ye unto it* (Num xxi, 17) . . . How was the well constructed? It was rock-shaped like a kind of bee-hive, and wherever they journeyed it rolled along and came with them" (Bamidbar Rabbah I.2).

Here as elsewhere, the Midrash adheres strictly to proof texts and at the same time provides extravagant supplements. If the well is attributed to Miriam, it is because she is always associated with water. In addition to her singing at the Red Sea, she has something to do, according to the rabbis, with the incantation by the well in Numbers 21:17. The rabbis rely on the similarity between the two occasions and above all on the recurrent use of the root *'anh* (sing). The fact that Miriam is already dead in Numbers 21 does not deter them from reaching this conclusion. On the contrary, the incantation is seen as proof that once Miriam dies, the well disappears and needs to be restored.

What is particularly interesting about this portable well is that it offers a female counterpart to the pillars of cloud and fire which, according to biblical tradition, traveled with the children of Israel, guiding, guarding, and nourishing them throughout their wanderings.

I do not mean to turn the Midrash into a feminist response to the Bible. There is no comparison between the respective attentions Moses and Miriam receive in midrashic interpretations. Rather, I have evoked the Midrash to accentuate biblical heteroglossia. For a perceptive discussion of the midrashic use of biblical heteroglossia, see Boyarin (1990a: 51–80).

8. Leiman (1976:16–19) provides an extensive discussion on the biblical evidence concerning noncanonical texts.

2. Creation according to Eve

1. Elizabeth Cady Stanton, like other leading figures in the nineteenth-century women's rights movement, began her political career as an abolitionist, fighting, among other things, against biblical interpretations which presented slavery as divinely ordained. It was her frustration over the exclusion of women from certain activities of the Anti-Slavery movement (the 1840 convention in London in particular), that led her to initiate, with Lucretia Mott, the women's rights convention at Seneca Falls. For more on the life and work of Stanton, see DuBois (1981), Griffith (1984), and Banner (1980).

2. The NAWSA disavowed any connection with *The Woman's Bible.*

3. Quoted in Gifford (1985:28).

4. For more on the ongoing favoring of Genesis 2, see Phillips (1984).

5. When referring to the various waves of feminist criticism, I rely on the observations of Elaine Showalter in her introduction to *The New Feminist Criticism* (1985).

6. Athalya Brenner, Cheryl Exum, and Carol Meyers are three other influential feminist biblical scholars. Because of this chapter's limited scope, however, I am unable to analyze their approaches. See the Bibliography for a selected list of their works.

7. Trible has been rightly criticized for her ahistorical approach by both Fiorenza (1983) and Bal (1986).

8. Two important books within this trend are Robert Alter's *The Art of Biblical Narrative* (1981) and Meir Sternberg's *The Poetics of Biblical Narrative* (1985).

9. Of the numerous reviews of *The Book of J,* the most valuable ones, to my mind, are those of Alter (1990), Damrosch (1991), Friedman (1991), Ostriker (1991), and Stern (1991).

10. Bachofen's *Das Mutterrecht,* first published in Germany in 1861, greatly influenced thinkers as different as Nietzsche, Engels, and Freud. His work has also inspired various female scholars, from Helen

Diner, whose book *Mothers and Amazons* appeared in 1929, to contemporary feminist mythmakers such as Elizabeth Gould Davis and Carol Christ. Some of the applications of Bachofen's ideas are discussed in Chapters 3 and 5. Let me add that although Bachofen's discovery of a matriarchal era has been discredited for lack of proof, he remains a keen reader of myths and symbols and is one of the first scholars to regard such topics as worthy of investigation. Selected texts from Bachofen's work are available in English in Ralph Manheim's edition, *Myth, Religion, and Mother Right* (1967).

11. That Bloom is primarily interested in Yahweh he admits in an interview in the *New York Times*. When asked about his hypothesis concerning J's gender, Bloom answered: "It doesn't matter at all . . . I made a very bad mistake. I'm absolutely convinced on internal, literary, and psychological grounds that this is a woman writer, but I wish I hadn't said it, because it's become a red herring. It distracts from the important outrage of the book. What matters in the book, what ought to be debated . . . is the way that the Yahweh of the J writer is absolutely not the God of the Hebrew Bible as a whole" (Oct. 24, 1990).

12. Bloom's conflation of his own work and that of J is particularly interesting in the passage depicting his initial thoughts concerning J's femininity: "My starting point of wonder came when I heard yet once more the familiar contention of feminist criticism that my own theories of influence are patriarchal. Why, I reflected, are the portraits of the Patriarchs and of Moses so mixed, and even at moments so unfavorable, in what the older scholarship found to be the Yahwistic, or earliest, portion of the Pentateuch?" (p. 34). Note the strange transitions from Bloom's wondering about J's gender, to his depiction of the criticism leveled at his own theories, and then back to J. As David Damrosch wittily puts it, "so two feminist birds can be killed with one revisionist stone: not only is Bloom himself no sexist, but the founding document of patriarchal tradition is not patriarchal at all: no heroes, only heroines" (1991).

3. Beyond Genesis 3: The Politics of Maternal Naming

(An earlier version of this chapter appeared in *Hebrew University Studies of Literature and the Arts*, vol. 17, 1989.)

1. When defining Genesis 4:1–2 as the point in which such a discourse arises, I am referring to J alone. Considering narrative continuum, the first budding of this genre may be traced back to P's brief

statement about the *toledot* (begettings) of heaven and earth in Genesis 2:1. For more on genealogies and their function within this literary unit, see Westermann (1984:9–18), Fishbane (1979:28–29), and Fokkelman (1987:40–44).

2. There are about seventeen cases in the Bible where the name-giver is male; of these in only eight cases—marked *—is a naming-speech delivered: Genesis 2:23*; 3:21*; 4:26; 5:3; 5:29*; 16:15; 21:3; 35:18; 41:51*, 52*; Exodus 18:3*, 4*; Judges 8:31; Job 42:14 (Job names his three daughters in one verse); 1 Chronicles 7:23*. There are twenty-seven cases of female name-givers and a higher ratio of maternal naming-speeches—66 percent (eighteen speeches): Genesis 4:1*, 25*; 16:11* (following God's request); 19:37, 38; 29:32*, 33*, 34*, 35*; 30:6*, 8*, 11*, 13*, 18*, 20*, 21, 24*; 35:18 (both Jacob and Rachel name Benjamin); 38:4, 5; Exodus 2:22*, Judges 13:24; 1 Samuel 1:20*; 1 Samuel 4:21*; 2 Samuel 12:24 (corrected text); 1 Chronicles 4:98; 1 Chronicles 7:16. Although in Isaac's case Abraham is the name-giver (Gen. 21:3), Sarah seems to be the one who interprets the name or delivers the naming-speech: "And Sarah said, God hath made me to laugh, so that all that hear will laugh with me. And she said, Who would have said unto Abraham, that Sarah should have given children suck? for I have born him a son in his old age" (Gen. 21:6–7*). Sarah's poetic speech may be defined, in Zakovitch's terms (1980), as an "implicit name-derivation."

3. In the spirit of French feminism, with its focus on the concept of *jouissance*, Bal suggests that the name "Eve" initiates a split between sexuality and motherhood. The first woman, who initially represented both sexuality and motherhood, is "condemned to predict Mary" upon receiving a name which stresses her maternal role alone. In Bal's hands, Eve's Fall becomes a witty inversion of the traditional perception of the Original Fall: sexuality is not discovered, but lost! Yet Bal's deconstruction of Christian mythology entails a problematic perpetuation of Christian concepts. Sexuality and motherhood go hand in hand for Eve in Genesis 4:1, as is usually the case in the Hebrew Bible. The Christian linking of sexuality, sin, and guilt (which creates the need to dissociate procreation from sexuality) is foreign to the Yahwistic text. For more on the difference between the respective Jewish and Christian perceptions of sexuality, see Pagels (1988) and Boyarin (forthcoming).

4. Transliterations in parentheses are my own.

5. See Alter (1981:67–69) and Sternberg (1985:97).

6. For more on the use of this formula in biblical narrative, both in the naming of characters and of places, see Long (1968).

7. For an analysis of phonetic association in naming-speeches, see Garsiel (1987).

8. Perhaps because it is self-explanatory, Eve does not comment upon her second son's name. "Abel," meaning "nothingness," is a proleptic name which foreshadows its bearer's untimely death. It is a shadowy counterpart of the creativity embodied in "Cain." (I am indebted to Chayuta Gurevich for calling my attention to this latter point.)

9. In this respect I disagree with Kikawada's suggestion that Genesis 4:1 is "a humble expression of the mother Eve" (1972:37). In his otherwise illuminating comparison of Mami's declaration of dependence on Enki in her creation of man to Eve's speech, he fails to consider the very different context within which Eve's words are spoken.

10. I am using Ben-Porat's terms (1976).

11. For more on the various ways in which the second verset in a parallelism may intensify the first, see Alter (1985) and Kugel (1981). Relying on Cassuto's observation that Lamech's triumphal song in Genesis 4:23—"For I have slain a man [*'ish*] to my wounding, a young man [*yeled*] to my hurt"—is an antithetic parallelism to Eve's poetic naming in Genesis 4:1 (p. 242), I have used *'ish* and *yeled* (boy) in Eve's case as well. (The King James translation of *yeled* is inaccurate; see Alter 1985:11–12.)

12. On the work of condensation, see Freud's seminal analysis in *The Interpretation of Dreams,* especially his consideration of verbal manifestations of condensation.

13. Job, who names his three daughters, is another fascinating exception. In Job's case, however, no naming-speeches are delivered. I discuss this matter in Chapter 8.

14. The quotation appears in Freud's letter to Jung (1974:288), where he endorses Otto Rank's suggestions. Roheim (1940) further analyzes Adam's Oedipal desires in "The Garden of Eden."

15. The lack of consideration of the mother's subjectivity is rooted in psychoanalytic theory. For more on this issue, see Suleiman (1985:352–377).

16. The significant difference between Eve's speeches is given an interesting twist in rabbinic interpretations. While Cain is considered the product of Eve's intercourse with the serpent (PRE, ch. 21), Seth is associated with the Messiah (see Breshit Rabba).

17. An analogous case which may clarify this issue is David's punishment in 2 Samuel 12:11. The strife characterizing the house of David is construed as punishment for David's sin, even though each one of David's sons has independent motives for his deeds.

18. My analysis of the interrelations between the Yahwistic and Priestly strands is informed by Damrosch's (1987) insightful literary-historical examination of this topic.

19. There are only three incidents of naming in P, and in all the father is the name-giver (Gen. 5:3; 16:15; 21:3). E. B. Cross sees the prominent role of mothers in naming in J as an indication that "the Hebrews passed through a stage in which kinship was reckoned through the mother rather than the father." According to Cross, the matronymic system was eventually replaced by a patronymic one, which explains the lack of female name-givers in P (1927:1–38). The fact that there are fathers, though relatively few, who name their sons in J refutes his observation. Cross, like Fromm and many other scholars of his time, applies Bachofen's speculative observations to the Bible. His analysis, however, is illuminating in its consideration of the differences between J and P in the realm of naming.

20. The division of the biblical text into chapters was not established until the thirteenth century.

21. See the polemic statements of Perry and Sternberg in their rejoinder "Zehirut Sifrut" (1970:631). Responding to the accusation that they have uncritically accepted the superimposed division into chapters in their analysis of the story of David and Bathsheba, Perry and Sternberg suggest that textual demarcation is as problematic in modern texts as in the Bible. Faulkner's work is but one of their examples.

4. Rachel's Dream: The Female Subplot

1. My approach to patriarchal specular dynamics thus differs from that of Luce Irigaray. In *Speculum* Irigaray suggests that woman is outside of representation in Western culture. She is the negative required by the male subject's specularization, the Other whose main function is to bolster the "subject's" position; she is "his faithful polished mirror, empty of altering reflections" (1985:136). Irigaray's critique of Western thought, though persuasive, fails to take into account the heterogeneity of specular dynamics.

2. For a beautiful comparison of the two "bed tricks," see Zvi Jagendorf (1984).

3. As Robert Alter argues, the annunciation type-scene is constructed upon a tripartite schema: initial barrenness; divine intervention; and the birth of a son. In some cases, "the distress of the barren wife is accented by the presence of a fertile, less loved co-wife" (1983:119; see Gen. 22; 1 Sam. 1).

4. For an illuminating analysis of the function of the *ficelle,* see Hochman (1985:86–89).

5. My reading of Rachel's dream as an unfulfilled dream owes much to Adin Steinsaltz's reading of her story (1984:49–54).

6. For an analysis of the mandrakes story, see Shinan and Zakovitch (1985).

7. Mieke Bal provides an extensive analysis of the transition from a patrilocal system to a virilocal one in *Death and Dissymmetry* (pp. 84–86 in particular). Her point of departure is Julius Morgenstern's study of the *beena* marriage in the Bible. The *beena* marriage, which was often practiced by nomads, entailed the following arrangement: the younger man, who had no fixed dwelling, tended the flocks of his father-in-law, whose house served as the center of power and wealth. Correcting Morgenstern's association of the *beena* marriage with matriarchy, Bal uses the term patrilocal, which makes clear that even though this system attributes much power to the bride's family, the focus on male authority remains. The virilocal marriage is opposed to patrilocal marriage insofar as the power is in the hands of the husband, who has the right to take his wife to his own clan.

8. See Pirke de Rabbi Eliezer 36; Agadat Breshit 51, Tanhuma, *parashat va-yetse.*

9. The story of Jephthah is well known: "Jephthah vowed a vow unto the Lord, and said, If thou shalt without fail deliver the children of Ammon into mine hands, Then it shall be, that whatsoever cometh forth of the doors of my house to meet me, when I return in peace from the children of Ammon, shall surely be the Lord's, and I will offer it up for a burnt offering" (Judg. 11:30–31). The first "thing" he ends up meeting, upon his triumphal return, is his own daughter. Bath-Jephthah thus becomes the victim of her father's speech act. Mieke Bal perceptively suggests that, "If we use the well-known realistic-psychological argument, we may say that this ritual [of women greeting the victor with dance and song] was well enough known for Jephthah to possibly have been aware of the risk he was taking; but obviously, his unawareness is precisely the point" (1988b:45).

10. Michal is another example of a rebellious daughter whose end is rather tragic. In a fascinating evocation of Rachel's move, Michal covers David's escape from her father's eyes by placing the household gods *(terafim)* in bed. Later, however, she is rejected by David and disappears from the stage (2 Sam. 6). For more on Michal and David, see Alter (1981:114–130).

11. I am grateful to Jonathan Rosen for this last point.

12. Roland Barthes (1977) offers an outstanding analysis of Jacob's struggle and transformation in Genesis 32.

13. Jacob is tricked by his sons, who present him with Joseph's stained coat, claiming that their brother has been devoured.

5. Zipporah and the Struggle for Deliverance

1. In this case, because of the inaccuracy of the King James Version, I have chosen to use the JPS translation. Unless otherwise indicated, future biblical citations will be from the King James Version.

2. Trible (1976:221) defines female subversiveness in the opening chapters of Exodus as an exemplary "depatriarchalized" element. Although I agree with the thrust of her argument, I find her premise that such elements prove that "the God of Israel defies sexism" inappropriate. See my critique of Trible in Chapter 2. For more on the role of women in Exodus 1–2, see Exum (1983) and Zeligs (1986).

3. For an analysis of Moses' role as one who "draws out," see Alter (1981:57–58).

4. Freud in fact develops his notion of "family romance" in relation to Moses' history in the first part of *Moses and Monotheism*. Following Otto Rank's thesis in *The Myth of the Birth of the Hero,* he suggests that the hero is one who stands up against his father and eventually overcomes him. In overcoming Pharaoh (a father figure for Moses in Freud's account), Moses proves himself a hero. While Freud's depiction of the father-son dyad is quite convincing, his lack of attention to the mother's role needs to be corrected. For a keen critique of the Freudian "family romance," see Neumann (1970).

5. Trickery is the topic of a special issue of *Semeia* (1988), edited by Cheryl Exum, entitled, "Reasoning with the Foxes: Female Wit in a World of Male Power." Mieke Bal's "Tricky Thematics" is especially insightful insofar as it does not limit trickery to women alone, but broadens the concept to include other oppressed groups that tend to make use of trickery.

6. The similarities between "The Bridegroom of Blood" and the story of Jacob's struggle have been noticed by many. For a particularly interesting comparison, see Buber (1988).

7. Perhaps Yahweh contributes to the confusion. If less plausible, He may be the one whose feet are touched.

8. Israel, as Moshe Greenberg suggests, is a late-born nation, which came "onto the stage only after all its neighbors had already assumed their historical roles" (1969:12). I would add that God may

treat Israel as a "firstborn" (Exod. 4:23), but this is but another manifestation of the reversal of the primogeniture law on the national level. My analysis of the unexpected victory of the weak in Exodus 4 owes much to Roland Barthes's (1977) fascinating reading of "Jacob's struggle with the Angel."

9. For a critique of the linking of *hatan* to *hatana,* see Childs (1974:97).

10. More recently, in *The Book of J,* Bloom goes so far as to suggest that J may have relied on an "archaic Judaism" unknown to us (1990:33), but his comments on this topic are brief and vague. His underlying premise is the same: J is strong to the point of nullifying prior traditions. Literary struggles take place between the Yahwistic text and its descendants—not its precursors.

11. Meyer's interpretation as a whole is one of the wildest readings of "The Bridegroom of Blood." He suggests that the nocturnal attack takes place during the bridal night of Zipporah and Moses. The demonic god claims the right of the *prima nox* for himself. Zipporah tricks "the lustful monster" by throwing Moses' foreskin at the demon's sexual organs; and the magical formula which she repeats is meant to confirm the fact that the demon has had the honor of being her first sexual partner. For more on the demonic character of this story, see Avishur (1980).

12. Howard Eilberg-Schwartz (1990:141–176) provides a fascinating anthropological study in which he shows that, contrary to what scholars often assume, the function of circumcision in biblical texts has much in common with the role of this rite in so-called "savage religions." He focuses on the association of circumcision with male fertility.

13. For a critique of the Midianite theories, see Childs (1974, 98; 328–332).

14. In depicting this myth I have relied on Bleeker (1963), Budge (1904), Frankfort (1948), Lexikon de Agyptologie, and Ochshorn (1981). I have also benefited greatly from conversations with Miriam Lichtheim and Irene Shirun-Grumach. Needless to say, responsibility for the views expressed remains entirely mine.

15. Text in Miriam Lichtheim's *Ancient Egyptian Literature* (1976: 83); bracketed explanations are mine.

16. Relying on postbiblical texts, Irene Shirun-Grumach (1983:7) draws the same conclusion. She points out that the name Josephus uses to designate Pharaoh's daughter—"Thermuthis"—is associated in Ptolemaic times with Isis. It is also noteworthy that the word used to depict Moses' ark in Exodus 2—*teva*—is an Egyptian word meaning coffer,

chest, holy shrine, coffin. Such chests, arks, or coffins were commonly carried on ships as part of a ceremonial reenactment of Osiris' casting into the Nile.

17. Isis' ruse is especially palpable when she tricks Seth in an attempt to ensure Horus' position as heir. Assuming the form of a beautiful woman, she entices Seth away from court and tells him of the miseries which befell her upon her husband's death: a stranger stole her son's inheritance. Seth's righteous anger is immediately turned against him once the goddess reveals her true identity.

18. For a critique of feminist "Goddess worship," see Paula Fredriksen Landes (1980). Freud's notion of spiritual progress has been challenged by Jonathan Culler (1982:59). I would like to add a few words about Freud's mistaken presuppositions in the passage quoted. First, the Mosaic prohibition against images does not imply that God is invisible. God's image may not be duplicated, nor can it be seen commonly, but it is nonetheless visible. The invisibility of the monotheistic God is but a Platonic misreading, which has become rooted in Western thought (see Boyarin 1990b). Second, names are not necessarily a paternal discourse. As I have shown in Chapter 3, more often than not it is the mother or the mother surrogate who names the child in biblical texts. Freud seems to ignore this fact, not only here but also in the opening pages of *Moses and Monotheism,* where he robs Pharaoh's daughter of her role as name-giver and attributes the naming of Moses to his Egyptian father.

19. For more on the stylistic differences between polytheistic texts and biblical texts, see Alter (1981:23–46).

20. The common argument, rightly criticized by Bal (1988b), according to which women are excluded from history because they are private figures who have no say in public affairs is proven wrong in the Bible, where the private and the public intermingle in unexpected ways. Although the acts of the female figures in Exodus (with the exception of the midwives) do not, strictly speaking, take place in the political realm, they serve as models for national deliverance and thus have an essential historical function. This by no means implies that these women are allotted central roles in the history of the house of Israel, but rather that their contribution to this history is unmistakable.

21. For qualifications of the instructive if overdrawn opposition between polytheistic and monotheistic texts in the ancient Near East—along the line of myth vs. history—see Albrektson (1967) and Damrosch (1987).

22. My understanding of such longings for previous cultural prac-

tices owes much to Stephen Greenblatt's discussions of this issue in *Shakespearean Negotiations,* especially his chapter on exorcism (1988:94–128).

23. Raphael Patai's argument in *The Hebrew Goddess* (1967) is at times overstated and at times far-fetched, but I agree with his major hypothesis concerning the Israelites' longing for a divine female deity.

24. In this case I use the new JPS translation because of its accurate rendition of the tone of Moses' complaint.

6. The Book of Ruth: Idyllic Revisionism

1. The verb "to build" *(bnh)* in biblical Hebrew means both "to construct" and "to bear children."

2. In Genesis, God blesses Sarah, saying that "she shall be a mother of nations; kings of people shall be of her" (17:16). Rebekah is blessed in a similar manner: "Thou art our sister, be thou the mother of thousands of millions, and let thy seed possess the gate of those which hate them" (Gen. 24:60). Yet the blessing of the matriarchs does not acquire a matrilineal momentum until one reaches the Book of Ruth.

3. B. M. Vellas' precursor is Herman Gunkel (1913). In a critique of political readings of the Book of Ruth, he teasingly provides the only message such a "charming" and idyllic text may be conveying: "men, beware of beautiful and intelligent women who want to have things their way." The tendency to define the Book of Ruth as an idyll owes much to the influence of Goethe's famous depiction of this text. Goethe regards the Book of Ruth as an idyll of great artistic value, "the loveliest little whole" in the Bible.

4. Ezra and Nehemiah set out to rid the nation of mixed marriages. In fact they go as far as to demand that all foreign wives be sent away (Ezra 9–10; Neh. 13). But the negative approach to foreign women prevails in other texts as well. For example, in Proverbs one finds the following warning: "For the lips of a strange woman drop as an honeycomb, and her mouth is smoother than oil: But her end is bitter as wormwood, sharp as a two-edged sword" (5:3–4). More relevantly, there is a law in Deuteronomy which forbids marriage with Moabites: "An Ammonite or Moabite shall not enter into the congregation of the Lord . . . Because they met you not with bread and with water in the way, when ye came forth out of Egypt" (23:3–4). The Book of Ruth, however, is not the only text which offers a positive representation of a foreign woman. Tamar (whose history is evoked in

the Book of Ruth), Pharaoh's daughter, Zipporah, and Yael are other notable examples.

5. Mieke Bal misses this point in her reading of The Book of Ruth (1987:68–88). Using Lacan's interpretation of Hugo's poem as a point of departure, she devotes much time to the implied impotence of Boaz and what Ruth can offer him in this respect, overlooking the antithetical construction of female heroism in this text.

6. For an analysis of the interrelations of the stories of Ruth, Tamar, and Lot's daughters, see Fisch (1982).

7. For more on antithetical completion, see Bloom (1984).

8. My analysis of the relationship of the mother-in-law and the daughter-in-law draws on Freud's depiction in *Totem and Taboo* (1957:14–16) of the ambivalence which marks the relationship of the mother-in-law and the son-in-law.

9. One such case in the male realm is the relationship of Moses and Jethro. Jethro is the father Moses never really had, a father figure from whom he learns a great deal about leadership.

10. In "Dora and the Pregnant Madonna" (1986) Mary Jacobus offers a perceptive analysis of the triangular dynamics in Dora's case, focusing on what Freud relegated to a footnote: Dora's love for Frau K.

11. There are two laws at stake in the Book of Ruth: the law of redemption and the law of levirate. The law of redemption obliges the closest kinsman of an impoverished person to redeem the land that the latter is forced to sell (see Lev. 25:23). This law both provides a type of social security and enables the preservation of land within the family. The law of levirate requires the brother of a deceased man to marry the widow if she is childless (see Deut. 25:5). It is meant to protect the widow and, above all, to ensure the posterity of the dead, for the child born of that union is to be named after the dead. In the Book of Ruth the two laws are inextricably connected, which is why Boaz is called redeemer in reference to both laws. For more on legal problems in the Book of Ruth, see Campbell (1975).

12. Mieke Bal (1987: 84–85) points to some of the intertextual ties between the Book of Ruth and the story of the mandrakes, but her analysis is problematic at two points. First, her suggestion that the allusion to Genesis is an unconscious one—for the people at the gate couldn't possibly have wanted to hurt Boaz by linking his case to the shameful story of the mandrakes—is unconvincing. The people at the gate, I believe, allude to Genesis precisely because they wish to underscore familial continuity. They attempt to naturalize the problematic aspects of the bond between Boaz and Ruth by intimating that the

house of Israel was "built"—from the very beginning—through curious, yet necessary, deviations. (The story of Tamar and Judah is another fine example.) The past, in other words, is invoked in order to empower and consecrate the marital union of Ruth and Boaz. Second, Bal fails to consider the differences between the respective representations of female bonding in Genesis and the Book of Ruth. She overlooks the fact that the momentary cooperation of Rachel and Leah in the story of the mandrakes is antithetically developed in the story of Ruth and Naomi.

13. Cynthia Ozick (1987) offers an extensive depiction of the opposition set up in this text between conventional behavior and singular choices.

14. In "Mourning and Melancholia" Freud mentions several features the two phenomena share: "profoundly painful dejection, cessation of interest in the outside world, loss of the capacity to love" (1957:244). He goes on to suggest that "the melancholic displays something else besides which is lacking in mourning—an extraordinary diminution in his self-regard, an impoverishment of his ego on a grand scale. In mourning it is the world which has become poor and empty; in melancholia it is the ego itself" (p. 246).

15. Athalya Brenner (1988) points to this split annunciation typescene and suggests that The Book of Ruth is a patchwork of Ruth's story and Naomi's story. Although I agree with her premise that there is a doubling of the female subject in this case, I do not find it necessary to attribute this phenomenon to a split origin.

16. My use of the concepts "voice" and "body" is informed by Elaine Scarry's *The Body in Pain* (1985).

17. For more on the prophetic association of barrenness and exile, see Callaway (1986) and Talmon (1988).

18. I am indebted to Galit Hazan-Rokem for drawing my attention to this midrash and sharpening my understanding as to its function within Lamentations Rabba.

7. *The Song of Songs and the Question of Canonization*

1. In dating the closing of the canon somewhere between the first and second centuries C.E., I am relying on scholarly consensus. However, even this rough estimate has been challenged. For more on the various hypotheses in this respect, see Leiman (1976) and Barr (1983).

2. It is not accidental that the disputable texts pertain to Writings. Presumably the Pentateuch had already been regarded as sacred and

fixed much earlier—approximately in the fifth or fourth centuries
B.C.E.—and most of the Prophetic texts had become fixed by about
200 B.C.E. For an extensive discussion concerning the Talmudic and
Midrashic evidence, see Leiman (1976).

3. This law was in the first instance applied to priests and not to
lay Jews.

4. The following exchange (quoted in Leiman 1976:107–108)
between Rabban Yohanan ben Zakkai, the Pharisee, and the Sadducees
illuminates the logic of attributing impurity to sacred objects. "The
Sadducees say: We have a quarrel to pick with you, O Pharisees, for
according to you the Holy Scriptures defile the hands whereas the writings of Homer would not defile the hands. Rabban Johanan ben Zakkai
replied: Have we naught against the Pharisees save this: According to
them the bones of an ass are clean while the bones of Johanan the High
Priest are unclean! They [the Sadducees] answered him: Their uncleanness corresponds to their preciousness, so that no man would make
spoons out of the bones of his father and mother. He [ben Zakkai] said
to them: So too the Holy Scriptures, their uncleanness corresponds to
their preciousness. The writings of Homer, which are not precious, do
not defile the hands" (M. Yadayim 4:6).

5. I am relying on Leiman's definition of canonicity. According
to Leiman, "a canonical book is a book accepted by the Jews as authoritative for religious practice and/or doctrine, and whose authority is
binding upon the Jewish people for all generations" (1976:14). For more
on the significance of binding, see Bruns (1984).

6. See BT *Sanhedrin,* 101a; *Tosefta, Sanhedrin,* 12:10, in the name
of R. Akiva.

7. Canonical criticism, as exemplified by Brevard Childs (1979)
and James Sanders (1984), has sought to underline the final shape of the
biblical text and highlight the unity brought about by redaction.

8. My understanding of this phenomenon owes much to
Kaufmann's seminal discussion in *The Religion of Israel* (1972) and to
Boyarin's insightful analysis of the corporeality or visibility of God
(1990).

9. For more on the development of the metaphor concerning
the amorous bond between Israel and God, see Cohen (1966) and
Greenberg (1983:292–306).

10. Fisch (1988:148–149) offers an interesting analysis of the
monotheistic reshaping of the Sacred Marriage Rite.

11. Considerable archaeological evidence suggests that popular
religion did not cease to endorse sexual rites until the Babylonian Exile

(see Patai 1967). But of course we can simply trust the prophets themselves, who complain time and again about the stubbornness of the people in this respect. Ezekiel's critical depiction of "the women weeping for Tammuz" at the gate of the Lord's house (8:14) is particularly relevant.

12. A number of critics, following the lead of T. J. Meek, have seen the Song as a cult liturgy connected with the celebration of the Sacred Marriage Rite. While such a reading has the beneficial results of evoking the background against which the Song was composed, it fails to account for the differences.

13. Kramer's translation (Wolkstein and Kramer 1983:108).

14. I have somewhat simplified matters in relating to this verse as a figurative statement. The lover's entrance to the garden may be understood both as a literal event and as a figurative depiction of an erotic encounter. I will elaborate on the complex interplay between literal and figurative sites and actions later.

15. I do not mean to suggest that such figuration is absent in the Sumerian corpus. In fact Kramer (1969) and Pope (1977) have pointed to the similarity in metaphoric play in the respective biblical and Sumerian representations of love. The garden is one such element. Much like the lovers in the Song, Inanna and Dumuzi often endow the garden in which they meet with figurative-erotic connotations.

He has brought me into it, he has brought me into it.
My brother has brought me into the garden.
Dumuzi has brought me into the garden . . .
I stood with him by its lying trees,
By an apple tree I kneeled as is proper . . .
I poured out plants from my womb,
I placed plants before him, I poured out plants before him.

(Kramer 1969:101)

Yet such figuration is already more explicit in its sexual implications (the womb turns out to be the source of the plants) and, as we have seen, is accompanied by literal depictions of sexual union. For an extensive discussion of the garden imagery in Sumerian and Babylonian texts, see Lambert (1987).

16. See Josipovici's (1988) comparison of the respective Hebrew and Christian perceptions of fulfillment. My understanding of the frustration of fulfillment in the Song is informed by Landy (1983) and Kristeva (1987).

17. In his sensitive commentary on the Song, Rashi underscores

the special consolatory power of this text. To his mind, "Solomon (fore)saw by the Holy Spirit, that Israel would be carried into one exile after another and would suffer one calamity after another; that in exile they would lament their former glory and remember the former love which God had shown them above all other nations . . . Hence Solomon produced this book by divine inspiration in the language of a woman saddened by a living widowhood, longing for her love . . . Her lover is saddened by her sorrow and remembers the loyalty of her youth, the charms of her beauty, and her good works which bound him to her with an everlasting love" (see Pope 1977:102–103).

18. Harold Fisch, who sees the dialogue in the Song as compatible with the dialogism found in the prophetic "conjugal trope" (1988: 101–102), misses this point. Here as elsewhere in his analysis of the Song, he points to intertextual ties in order to stress the unity of Holy Writ and thus overlooks the Song's antithetical character. This is particularly disturbing in his suggestion that the Song could be read as "a love poem addressed to a beloved land" (p. 92). Instead of analyzing the ways the Song inverts the prophetic female personification of the land—by turning Jerusalem (as well as other sites) into a vehicle which depicts the beloved—Fisch finds symmetry in such intertextuality, a symmetry which enables him to attribute to the Song a prophetic mode of nationalism.

19. I am grateful to Rei Masui, whose analysis (in an unpublished paper) of the male groups in the Song has sharpened my understanding of the patriarchal dimension in this text.

20. The repression of female eroticism or its misrepresentation in Western culture has been a topic of much interest in feminist theory. For representative works on this issue, see Irigaray (1985) and Suleiman (1986).

21. My understanding of this phenomenon owes much to Alter's illuminating analysis in *The Art of Biblical Poetry* (1985).

22. My reading of this passage as a possible depiction of an auto-erotic event is informed by Chana Kronfeld's beautiful analysis in "Beyond Language Pangs" (1990).

23. I have relied on the observations of Fokkelien van Dijk-Hemmes (1992) in my discussion of the difference between the Song and Hosea with respect to focalization.

24. For more on the use of military architecture in the Song, see Carol Meyers (1986).

25. My understanding of the different perceptions of virginity in

the Song is informed by Mieke Bal's analysis of virginity in *Death and Dissymmetry,* particularly the chapter on Bath-Jephthah, entitled "Virginity and Entanglement" (1988b:41–68).

26. See Diane Wolkstein's analysis of Inanna's maturation (1983: 137–146).

8. Conclusion

1. I am endebted to Katherine Clay Bassard, whose paper, "Poetic Silence: En-gendered Suffering in the Book of Job" (MLA, November 1990), increased my understanding of the role of Job's wife.

2. The talmudic sage Rava interpreted this verse in a similar way: "with his lips he sinned not, but in his heart he did!" (Babylonian Talmud, Bava Batra 16a).

3. My understanding of the transformation Job undergoes is informed by Jack Kahn's fascinating psychological interpretation of Job's character in *Job's Illness: Loss, Grief, and Integration* (1975).

4. Robert Alter (1981:126–127) offers an insightful analysis of the flexible use of epithets in the Bible.

5. René Girard (1987) examines Job's sense of being persecuted and suggests that his fate resembles that of a scapegoat. Girard's analysis is insightful where the question of Job's isolation is concerned, but he fails to take into account Job's own contribution to his solitary position.

6. Dinah is the only other daughter whose naming is recounted. In this case, however, the name-giver is the mother, Leah (Gen. 30:21).

7. Interestingly, the Voice from the Whirlwind contributes to Job's admiration of beauty insofar as it opens his eyes to the unfathomable beauty of creation. For a discussion of this matter, see Alter (1985:85–110).

8. The law concerning the inheritance of daughters is discussed in Numbers 27:1–8.

9. The question of debates within feminist criticism has been tackled from various angles in a recently published collection entitled *Conflicts In Feminism* (1990), edited by Marianne Hirsch and Evelyn Fox Keller.

10. For more on the "mother's house," see Carol Meyers (1991).

Bibliography

Ackerman, James. 1974. "The Literary Context of the Moses Birth Story." In *Literary Interpretations of Biblical Narratives,* ed. K. R. Gros Louis. Nashville, Tenn.: Abingdon, 1:74–119.

Albrektson, Bertil. 1967. *History and the Gods: An Essay on the Idea of Historical Events as Divine Manifestations in the Ancient Near East and Israel.* Lund: Gleerup.

Alter, Robert. 1981. *The Art of Biblical Narrative.* New York: Basic Books

———. 1983. "How Convention Helps Us Read: The Case of the Bible's Annunciation Type-Scene." *Prooftexts* 3:115–130.

———. 1985. *The Art of Biblical Poetry.* New York: Basic Books.

———. 1990. "Harold Bloom's 'J'." Review of *The Book of J,* by Harold Bloom. *Commentary* (November), 28–33.

Anderson, Francis I., and David Noel Freedman. 1980. *Hosea.* The Anchor Bible. Garden City, N.Y.: Doubleday.

Auerbach, Erich. 1974 (1946). *Mimesis: The Representation of Reality in Western Literature.* Trans. Willard Trask. Princeton: Princeton University Press.

Avishur, Yitzhak. 1980. "Leofyo Hademony Shel Sipur Hatan Damim." *Eshel Beer Sheva,* vol. 2 (in Hebrew).

Bachofen, J. J. 1967. *Myth, Religion, and Mother Right: Selected Writings of J. J. Bachofen.* Trans. Ralph Manheim. Bollingen 84. Princeton: Princeton University Press.

Bakhtin, M. M. 1981. *The Dialogic Imagination.* Ed. Michael Holquist, trans. Caryl Emerson and Michael Holquist. Austin: University of Texas Press.

————. 1984. *Problems of Dostoevsky's Poetics*. Ed. and trans. Caryl Emerson. Minneapolis: University of Minnesota Press.

Bal, Mieke. 1986. "The Bible as Literature: A Critical Escape." *Diacritics* (Winter), 71–79.

————. 1987. *Lethal Love: Feminist Literary Interpretations of Biblical Love Stories*. Bloomington: Indiana University Press.

————. 1988a. *Murder and Difference: Gender, Genre and Scholarship on Sisera's Death*. Bloomington: Indiana University Press.

————. 1988b. *Death and Dissymmetry: The Politics of Coherence in the Book of Judges*. Chicago: The University of Chicago Press.

————. 1988c. "Tricky Thematics." *Semeia* 42:133–155.

Banner, Lois W. 1980. *Elizabeth Cady Stanton*. Boston: Little Brown and Company.

Barr, James. 1983. *Holy Scripture: Canon, Authority, Criticism*. Oxford: Oxford University Press.

Barthes, Roland. 1977. "The Struggle With the Angel." In *Image, Music, Text,* trans. Stephen Heath. London: Fontana Collins, 125–141.

Beauvoir, Simone de. 1952 (1949). *The Second Sex*. Trans. H. M. Parshley. New York: Vintage Books.

Ben-Porat, Ziva. 1976. "The Poetics of Literary Allusion." *PTL* 1: 105–128.

Bettelheim, Bruno. 1962. *Symbolic Wounds, Puberty Rites, and the Envious Male*. New York: Collier Books.

Biale, Rachel. 1984. *Women and Jewish Law*. New York: Schocken Books.

Blau, Yehoshua. 1956. "Hatan Damim." *Tarbiz* 26:1–3 (in Hebrew).

Bleeker, C. J. 1963. "Isis as Saviour Goddess." In *The Saviour God: Comparative Studies in the Concept of Salvation Presented to Edwin Oliver James,* ed. S. G. F. Brandon. Manchester: Manchester University Press, 1–16.

Bloom, Harold. 1973. *The Anxiety of Influence: A Theory of Poetry*. New York: Oxford University Press.

————. 1982. Introduction. *On the Bible,* by Martin Buber. New York: Schocken Books.

————. 1984. "'Before Moses Was, I Am': The Original and the Belated Testaments." *Notebooks in Cultural Analysis,* I. Durham, N.C.: Duke University Press, 3–14.

————. 1990. *The Book of J*. Trans. David Rosenberg, interpreted by Harold Bloom. New York: Grove Weidenfeld.

Boyarin, Daniel. 1990a. *Intertextuality and the Reading of Midrash*. Bloomington: Indiana University Press.

————. 1990b. "The Eye in the Torah: Ocular Desire in Midrashic Hermeneutic." *Critical Inquiry* 16:532–549.

————. (Forthcoming.) *Carnal Israel: Reading Sex in Talmudic Culture*. Berkeley: University of California Press.

Brenner, Athalya. 1985. *The Israelite Woman: Social Role and Literary Type in Biblical Narrative*. Sheffield: JSOT Press.

————. 1988. *Ruth and Naomi: Literary, Stylistic and Linguistic Studies in the Book of Ruth*. Tel Aviv: Afik (in Hebrew).

Bruns, Gerald L. 1984. "Canon and Power in the Hebrew Scriptures." In *Canons*, ed. Robert Hallberg. Chicago: The University of Chicago Press, 65–83.

Buber, Martin. 1988 (1946). *Moses: The Revelation and the Covenant*. Atlantic Highlands, N.J.: Humanities Press International.

Budge, E. A. Wallis. 1904. *The Gods of the Egyptians*. London: Methuen.

Callaway, Mary. 1986. *Sing O Barren One: A Study in Comparative Midrash*. Atlanta: Scholars Press.

Campbell, E. F. 1975. *Ruth*. The Anchor Bible. Garden City, N.Y.: Doubleday & Company.

Cassuto, Umberto. 1961 (1944). *Commentary on Genesis I: From Adam to Noah*. Trans. Israel Abrahams. Jerusalem: Magnes Press.

————. 1967 (1951). *A Commentary on the Book of Exodus*. Trans. Israel Abrahams. Jerusalem: Magnes Press.

Childs, Brevard S. 1974. *The Book of Exodus: A Critical, Theological, Commentary*. Philadelphia: Westminster.

————. 1979. *Introduction to the Old Testament as Scripture*. Philadelphia: Fortress Press.

Christ, Carol, and Judith Plaskow, eds. 1979. *Womanspirit Rising*. Boston: Beacon Press.

Cohen, Gerson D. 1966. "The Song of Songs and the Jewish Religious Mentality." In *The Samuel Friedland Lectures 1960–66*. New York: Jewish Theological Seminary, 1–21.

Cross, E. B. 1927. *The Hebrew Family*. Chicago: Chicago University Press.

Culler, Jonathan. 1982. *On Deconstruction: Theory and Criticism After Structuralism*. Ithaca: Cornell University Press.

Daly, Mary. 1973. *Beyond God the Father: Toward a Philosophy of Women's Liberation*. Boston: Beacon Press.

Damrosch, David. 1987. *The Narrative Covenant: Transformations of Genre in the Growth of Biblical Literature*. San Francisco: Harper and Row.

————. 1991. "The Human From Divine." Review of *The Book of J*, by Harold Bloom. *The World & I* (February): 364–372.

Dijk-Hemmes, Fokkelien van. 1992. "The Imagination of Power and the Power of Imagination: An Intertextual Analysis of Two Biblical Lovesongs: The Song of Songs and Hosea 2." In *The Song of Songs: A Feminist Reader,* ed. Athalya Brenner. Sheffield: Sheffield Academic Press.

DuBois, Ellen Carol. 1981. *Elizabeth Cady Stanton, Susan B. Anthony: Correspondence, Writings, Speeches.* New York: Schocken Books.

Dundes, Alan. 1983. "Couvade in Genesis." In *Folklore Research Center Studies* 7:33–53.

Eilberg-Schwartz, Howard. 1990. *The Savage in Judaism: An Anthropology of Israelite Religion and Ancient Judaism.* Bloomington: Indiana University Press.

Empson, William. 1968. *Some Versions of Pastoral.* New York: New Directions.

Exum, Cheryl J. 1983. "'You Shall Let Every Daughter Live': A Study of Exodus 1:8–2:10." *Semeia* 28, 63–82.

————. ed. 1988. "Reasoning with the Foxes: Female Wit in a World of Male Power." *Semeia* 42.

Falk, Marcia. 1982. *Love Lyrics from the Bible.* Sheffield: The Almond Press.

Fiorenza, Elisabeth Schüssler. 1986. *In Memory of Her.* New York: Crossroad.

Fisch, Harold. 1982. "Ruth and the Structure of Covenant History." *Vetus Testamentum* 32:4, 425–437.

————. 1988. *Poetry with a Purpose: Biblical Poetics and Interpretation.* Bloomington: Indiana University Press.

Fishbane, Michael. 1979. *Text and Texture.* New York: Schocken Books.

Fokkelman, J. P. 1975. *Narrative Art in Genesis.* Amsterdam: Van Gorcum, Assen.

————. 1987. "Genesis." In *The Literary Guide to the Bible,* ed. Robert Alter and Frank Kermode. Cambridge, Mass.: Harvard University Press, 36–55.

Fontaine, Carole. 1988. "The Deceptive Goddess in Ancient Near Eastern Myth: Inanna and Inras." *Semeia* 42:84–102.

Frankfort, Henri. 1948. *Kingship and the Gods: A Study of Ancient Near Eastern Religion as the Integration of Society and Nature.* Chicago: The University of Chicago Press.

Freud, Sigmund. 1957 (1900). *The Interpretation of Dreams.* In vol. 4 of

The Standard Edition of the Complete Psychological Works of Sigmund Freud, ed. and trans. by James Strachey. London: The Hogarth Press Ltd.

———. 1957 (1913). *Totem and Taboo.* In vol. 13 of *The Standard Edition,* 1–162

———. 1957 (1917). "Resistance and Repression." In vol. 16 of *The Standard Edition,* 286–302.

———. 1957 (1917). "Mourning and Melancholia." In vol. 14 of *The Standard Edition*

———. 1958 (1908). "The Relation of the Poet to Day-Dreaming." In *On Creativity and the Unconscious: Papers on the Psychology of Art, Literature, Love, Religion,* trans. John Riviere. New York: Harper and Row.

———. 1967 (1939). *Moses and Monotheism.* Trans. Katherine Jones. New York: Vintage Books.

———. 1974. *The Freud/Jung Letters.* Princeton: Princeton University Press.

Friedman, R. E. 1991. "Is Everybody a Bible Expert?" Review of *The Book of J,* by Harold Bloom. *Bible Review* (April), 16–18, 50–51.

Fromm, Erich. 1951. *The Forgotten Language.* New York: Grove Press.

Fuchs, Esther. 1985a. "The Literary Characterization of Mothers and Sexual Politics in the Hebrew Bible." In *Feminist Perspectives on Biblical Scholarship,* ed. Adela Yarbro Collins. Chico, Calif.: Scholars Press, 117–136.

———. 1985b. "Who Is Hiding the Truth? Deceptive Women and Biblical Androcentrism." In *Feminist Perspectives on Biblical Scholarship,* ed. Adela Yarbro Collins, 137–144.

———. 1986a. "Structure and Patriarchal Functions in the Biblical Betrothal Type-Scene." *Journal of Feminist Studies and Religion* 3:1, 7–14.

———. 1986b. "Toward a Feminist Hermeneutics of Biblical Narrative." Paper presented at the annual convention of the Society of Biblical Literature.

———. 1988. "'For I Have the Way of Women': Deception, Gender, and Ideology in Biblical Narrative." *Semeia* 42:68–83.

Gallop, Jane. 1982. *The Daughter's Seduction: Feminism and Psychoanalysis.* Ithaca: Cornell University Press.

Garsiel, Moshe. 1987. *Midrashic Name Derivations in the Bible.* Tel-Aviv: Revivim (in Hebrew).

Gifford, Caroline De Swarte. 1985. "American Women and the Bible: The Nature of the Hermeneutical Issue." In *Feminist Perspectives on*

Biblical Scholarship, ed. Adela Yarbro Collins. Chico, Calif.: Scholars Press, 11–34.

Ginzburg, Christian D. 1970. *The Song of Songs and Coheleth,* New York: Ktav Publishing House.

Girard, René. 1977 (1972). *Violence and the Sacred.* Trans. Patrick Gregory. Baltimore: The John Hopkins University Press.

———. 1987 (1985). *Job: The Victim of His People,* trans. Yvonne Freccero. Stanford: Stanford University Press.

Greenberg, Moshe. 1969. *Understanding Exodus.* New York: Behrman House, Inc., for the Melton Research Center of the Jewish Theological Seminary of America.

———. 1983. *Ezekiel 1–20.* The Anchor Bible. Garden City, N.Y.: Doubleday.

———. 1987. "Job." In *The Literary Guide to the Bible,* ed. Robert Alter and Frank Kermode. Cambridge, Mass.: Harvard University Press, 283–304.

Greenblatt, Stephen. 1988. *Shakespearean Negotiations.* New York: Oxford University Press.

Griffith, Elisabeth. 1984. *In Her Own Right: The Life of Elizabeth Cady Stanton.* New York: Oxford University Press.

Gunkel, Hermann. 1913. "Ruth." In *Reden und Aufsatze,* 65–92.

———. 1964 (1901). *The Legends of Genesis: The Biblical Saga & History.* Trans. W. H. Carruth. New York: Schocken Books.

Gurevich, Zali. 1990. "The Embrace: On the Element of Non-Distance in Human Relations." *Sociological Quarterly* 31:2.

Hartman, Geoffrey H. 1986. "The Struggle for the Text." In *Midrash and Literature,* ed. G. Hartman and S. Budick. New Haven: Yale University Press, 3–18.

Hirsch, Marianne, and Evelyn Fox Keller, eds. 1990. *Conflicts in Feminism.* New York: Routledge.

Hochman, Baruch. 1985. *Character in Literature.* Ithaca: Cornell University Press.

Horney, Karen. 1967. *Feminine Psychology.* New York: W. W. Norton & Company.

Irigaray, Luce. 1985 (1974). *Speculum of the Other Woman.* Trans. G. Gill. Ithaca: Cornell University Press.

Irvin, Dorothy. 1977. "The Joseph and Moses Stories as Narrative in the Light of Ancient Near Eastern Narrative." In *Israelite and Judaean History,* ed. J. H. Hayes and J. M. Miller. London: SCM Press, 193–194.

Jacobus, Mary. 1986. *Reading Woman: Essays in Feminist Criticism.* New York: Columbia University Press.

Jagendorf, Zvi. 1984. "'In the Morning, Behold, It Was Leah': Genesis and the Reversal of Sexual Knowledge." In *Biblical Patterns in Modern Literature,* ed. David Hirsch and Nehama Ashkenazy. Providence: Brown University Press, 51–60.

James, Henry. 1986 (1881). *The Portrait of a Lady.* New York: Penguin Books.

Josipovici, Gabriel. 1988. *The Book of God: A Response to the Bible.* New Haven: Yale University Press.

Kahn, Jack. 1975. *Job's Illness: Loss, Grief and Integration.* Oxford: Pergamon Press.

Kaufmann, Ezekiel. 1972. *The Religion of Israel.* Trans. Moshe Greenberg. New York: Schocken Books.

Kikawada, Isaac M. 1972. "Two Notes on Eve." *JBL* 91:33–37.

Kosmala, Hans. 1962. "The 'Bloody Husband.'" *Vetus Testamentum* 12:14–28.

Kramer, Samuel Noah. 1969. *The Sacred Marriage Rite: Aspects of Faith, Myth, and Ritual in Ancient Sumer.* Bloomington: Indiana University Press.

Kristeva, Julia. 1987 (1983). *Tales of Love.* Trans. L. S. Roudiez. New York: Columbia University Press.

———. 1991 (1988). *Strangers to Ourselves.* Trans. L. S. Roudiez. New York: Columbia University Press.

Kronfeld, Chana. (Forthcoming.) "Beyond Language Pangs: The Stylistics of Modernism in Hebrew Poetry." In *The Renaissance of Hebrew in the Modern Age: Literature, Language, and Society,* ed. B. Harshav. Berkeley: University of California Press.

Kugel, James L. 1981. *The Idea of Biblical Poetry.* New Haven: Yale University Press.

Kuspit, Donald. 1989. "A Mighty Metaphor: The Analogy of Archaeology and Psychoanalysis." In *Sigmund Freud and Art: His Personal Collection of Antiques.* London: Thames and Hudson, Ltd., 133–152.

Lambert, W. G. 1987. "Devotion: The Languages of Religion and Love." In *Figurative Language in the Ancient Near East,* ed. M. Mindlin, M. J. Geller, and J. E. Wansbrough. London: School of Oriental and African Studies, 25–39.

Landes, Paula Fredriksen. 1980. Review. *Signs* 2:328–334.

Landy, Francis. 1983. *Paradoxes of Paradise: Identity and Difference in the Song of Songs.* Sheffield: The Almond Press.

Leach, Edmund. 1983. "Why Did Moses Have a Sister?" In *Structuralist Interpretations of Biblical Myth.* Cambridge: Cambridge University Press, 33–67.

Leiman, Sid Z. 1976. *The Canonization of Hebrew Scripture: The Talmudic and Midrashic Evidence.* Hamden, Conn.: Archon Books.

Lerner, Gerda. 1986. *The Creation of Patriarchy.* New York: Oxford University Press.

Levin, Richard. 1971. *The Multiple Plot in English Renaissance Drama.* Chicago: The University of Chicago Press.

Lichtheim, Miriam. 1976. *Ancient Egyptian Literature.* Vol. II: *The New Kingdom.* Berkeley: University of California Press.

Loewenstamm, Samuel E. 1972. *The Tradition of the Exodus in Its Development.* Jerusalem: Magnes Press (in Hebrew).

Long, B. O. 1968. *The Problem of Etiological Narrative in the O.T.* Berlin: Topelmann.

Meyer, Eduard. 1906. *Die Israeliten und ihre Nachbarstaemme.*

Meyers, Carol. 1986. "Gender and Imagery in the Song of Songs." *Hebrew Annual Review* 10:209–221.

———. 1988. *Discovering Eve: Ancient Israelite Women in Context.* New York: Oxford University Press.

———. (Forthcoming.) " 'To Her Mother's House': Considering a Counterpart to the Israelite *Bet 'ab.*" In *The Bible and the Politics of Exegesis.* New York: Pilgrim Press.

Miller, Nancy. 1981. "Emphasis Added: Plots and Plausibilities in Women's Fiction." *PMLA* 96:36–48.

Millett, Kate. 1969. *Sexual Politics.* New York: Ballantine.

Mitchell, Stephen. 1987. Introduction. *The Book of Job.* San Francisco: North Point Press.

Morgenstern, Julian. 1963. "The 'Bloody Husband'(?) (Exod. 4:24–26) Once Again." *Hebrew Union College Annual* 34:14–28.

Morson, G. S., and Caryl Emerson, eds. 1989. *Rethinking Bakhtin: Extensions and Challenges.* Evanston, Ill.: Northwestern University Press.

Neumann, Erich. 1970 (1949). *The Origins and History of Consciousness.* Bollingen Series XLII. Princeton: Princeton University Press.

Noth, Martin. 1968. *Numbers: A Commentary.* London: SCM Press.

Ochshorn, Judith. 1988. "Ishtar and Her Cult." In *The Book of the Goddesses: Past and Present.* New York: Crossroad, 16–28.

Ostriker, Alicia. 1991. "Liberated Theology." Review of *The Book of J,* by Harold Bloom. *Tikkun* 6:43–45.

Ozick, Cynthia. 1987. "Ruth." In *Congregation: Contemporary Writers Read the Jewish Bible,* ed. David Rosenberg. New York: Harcourt Brace Jovanovich, 361–382.

Pagels, Elaine. 1988. *Adam, Eve, and the Serpent*. New York: Random House.

Patai, Raphael. 1967. *The Hebrew Goddess*. New York: Ktav Publishing House.

Perry, Menakhem, and Meir Sternberg. 1970. "Zehirut Sifrut!" *Ha-Sifrut* 2:608–663 (in Hebrew).

Phillips, John A. 1984. *Eve: The History of an Idea*. San Francisco: Harper and Row.

Plaskow, Judith. 1990. *Standing Again at Sinai: Judaism from a Feminist Perspective*. San Francisco: Harper and Row.

Pope, Marvin H. 1977. *Song of Songs*. The Anchor Bible. Garden City, N.Y.: Doubleday.

Rank, Otto. 1932 (1914). *The Myth of the Birth of the Hero*. Trans. Mabel E. Moxon. New York: Vintage Books.

Rich, Adrienne. 1976. *Of Woman Born: Motherhood as Experience and Institution*. New York: Norton.

Rimmon-Kenan, Shlomith. 1983. *Narrative Fiction: Contemporary Poetics*. London: Methuen.

Roheim, Geza. 1940. "The Garden of Eden." *Psychoanalytic Review* 27, no. 1 (January): 1–26; no. 2 (April): 177–199.

Ruether, Rosemary Radford. 1983. *Sexism and God-Talk: Toward a Feminist Theology*. Boston: Beacon Press.

Sanders, James A. 1984. *Canon and Community: A Guide to Canonical Criticism*. Philadelphia: Fortress Press.

Sasson, Jack M. 1979. *Ruth*. Baltimore: The Johns Hopkins University Press.

Scarry, Elaine. 1985. *The Body in Pain: The Making and Unmaking of the World*. Oxford: Oxford University Press.

Shinan, Avigdor, and Yair Zakovitch. 1985. *The Story of the Mandrakes*. Jerusalem: Research Projects of the Institute of Jewish Studies Monograph Series 8. The Hebrew University (in Hebrew).

Shirun-Grumach, Irene. 1983. "Slow of Speech and Slow of Tongue: An Expressive Gesture." In *Norms and Variations in Art: Essays in Honour of Moshe Barasch*. Jerusalem: The Institute of Languages, Literatures and Art, Magnes Press, 3–12.

Showalter, Elaine. 1985. *The New Feminist Criticism: Essays on Women, Literature, and Theory*. New York: Pantheon Books.

Skinner, John. 1910. *Genesis*. The International Critical Commentary. Edinburgh: T. & T. Clark.

Speiser, E. A. 1964. *Genesis*. The Anchor Bible. Garden City, N.Y.: Doubleday.

Spretnak, Charlene, ed. 1982. *The Politics of Women's Spirituality: Essays on the Rise of Spiritual Power within the Feminist Movement.* Garden City, N.Y.: Anchor Books.

Stanton, Elizabeth Cady. 1985 (1895, 1898). *The Woman's Bible: The Original Feminist Attack on the Bible.* Edinburgh: Polygon Books.

Steinsaltz, Adin. 1984. *Biblical Images: Men and Women of the Book.* Trans. Yehuda Hanegbi and Yehudit Keshet. New York: Basic Books.

Stern, David. 1991. "The Supreme Fictionalist." Review of *The Book of J,* by Harold Bloom. *The New Republic* (Feb. 4), 34–40.

Sternberg, Meir. 1985. *The Poetics of Biblical Narrative: Ideological Literature and the Drama of Reading.* Bloomington: Indiana University Press.

Suleiman, Susan Rubin. 1985. "Writing and Motherhood." In *(M)other Tongue: Essays in Feminist Psychoanalytic Interpretation,* ed. Shirley Nelson Garner, Claire Kahane, and Madelon Spregnether. Ithaca: Cornell University Press, 352–377.

———. 1986. "(Re)Writing the Body: The Politics and Poetics of Female Eroticism." In *The Female Body in Western Culture,* ed. Susan Rubin Suleiman. Cambridge, Mass.: Harvard University Press, 7–29.

Talmon, Shemaryahu. 1954. "Hatan Damim." *Eretz Yisrael* 3:93–95 (in Hebrew).

———. 1988. "Literary Motifs and Speculative Thought in the Hebrew Bible." *HSLA* 16:150–168.

Trible, Phyllis. 1976. "Depatriarchalizing in Biblical Interpretation." In *The Jewish Woman: New Perspectives,* ed. Elizabeth Koltun. New York: Schocken Books, 217–240.

———. 1978. *God and the Rhetoric of Sexuality.* Philadelphia: Fortress Press.

———. 1989. "Bringing Miriam Out of the Shadows." *Bible Review* 5:14–25.

Vellas, B. M. 1954. "The Book of Ruth and its Purpose." *Theologia* (Athens) 25:201–210.

Weinfeld, Moshe. 1979. "Ha'el Habore." In *A Biblical Studies Reader,* ed. M. Weinfeld. Jerusalem: Magnes Press (in Hebrew), 117–146.

Westermann, Claus. 1984. *Genesis 1–11.* Trans. John Scullion. Minneapolis: Augsburg Publishing House.

Wolkstein, Diane, and Samuel Noah Kramer. 1983. *Inanna: Queen of Heaven and Earth.* New York: Harper & Row.

Woolf, Virginia. 1929. *A Room of One's Own*. New York: Harcourt Brace Jovanovich.

Zakovitch, Yair. "Explicit and Implicit Name-Derivations." *Hebrew Annual Review* 4:167–181.

Zeligs, Dorothy. 1986. *Moses: A Psychodynamic Study*. New York: Human Sciences Press.

Index